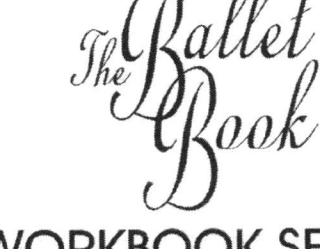

The Ballet Book

WORKBOOK SERIES

by Donna Jones Carver and Sally E. Weatherford

Illustrations by Amanda Shumway
Graphic Art by Karen F. Jeffiers

From The Authors:

Welcome to Workbook III. We invite you to use this workbook as a tool for learning more about ballet and its related areas. Each lesson and activity reflects proper form and accurate information. We think you'll find this book a valuable reference for history, anatomy, biographies, vocabulary and theory, as well as an in depth look at the classic ballets presented.
Illustrations are provided for all three schools, French, Russian and Cecchetti; the method preferred by your school can be emphasized. Vocabulary phonetics are an approximation of American pronunciations of the French words.
The Ballet Book Series has been created with the goal of helping young dancers gain more knowledge and understanding of their art.

With love and appreciation for their invaluable encouragement and support, we dedicate this series to Don W. Belcher, Stephen L. Edwards, Robert L. Fields, Royce F. Green, Mary McGavock, Jan and Ray Smith and, most especially, Lawson B. Jones.

Published by
Lewelyn & Company, LLC
P.O. Box 128045
Nashville, TN 37212

ISBN: 1-887707-02-6

To The Student

This workbook was not designed to teach you how to dance, or stress any one ballet technique over another, but to enhance your understanding of the art of ballet.

By taking you from ballet's earliest beginnings, through the lives of those who made its history, to modern times, this workbook will, hopefully, inspire you to search further and investigate deeper into the soul of ballet and its people. Although we are covering only ballet here, there are many other dance forms that hold interesting and fascinating information for you to discover.

The theory, anatomy, vocabulary, biographies, history and ballet presentations covered here are basic efforts to increase your education of the art of ballet and are not meant to convey that this is all there is to learn in these various areas.

We hope you enjoy using this workbook and have a good time learning more about ballet. But most of all, we hope your love for ballet will grow and enrich your life.

- The Authors

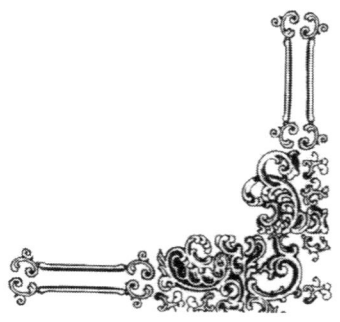

The Ballet Book

Lessons

Lesson One

1. In the space below draw, using circles, the Cinq Positions Des Pieds and name each one.

    (Feet)

    (Name) _____ _____ _____ _____ _____

2. In the space to the right, draw a square,
    and using either Cecchetti or Vaganova,
    mark the fixed points for the dancer and
    explain why this is used.

    _____

3. Name the three main schools of ballet technique.

    1._____ 2._____ 3._____

4. Read the biography of Fanny Elssler and answer the questions below:

    a. The qualities Elssler brought to her dancing were described as _____
       and _____ .

    b. The flames of a supposed rivalry between Fanny Elssler and _____
       were fanned by the Paris Opéra director, _____, who
       thought it would help sell tickets at the box office.

5. From where does the word "ballet" come? _____

6. What happened in Paris on October 15, 1581? _____

7. Read the ballet "La Fille Mal Gardée" and answer the following questions:

    a. First presented: Year _____ Place _____ .

    b. The two leading roles are named _____ and _____ .

    c. Madame Simone is what relation to the lead female role? _____

8.   a. The body is made up of more than 200 bones. (circle one)   True or False

b. Foot bones are called _____ and metacarpals are _____.

9.   Match the bone by writing the number on the line showing its location in the body.

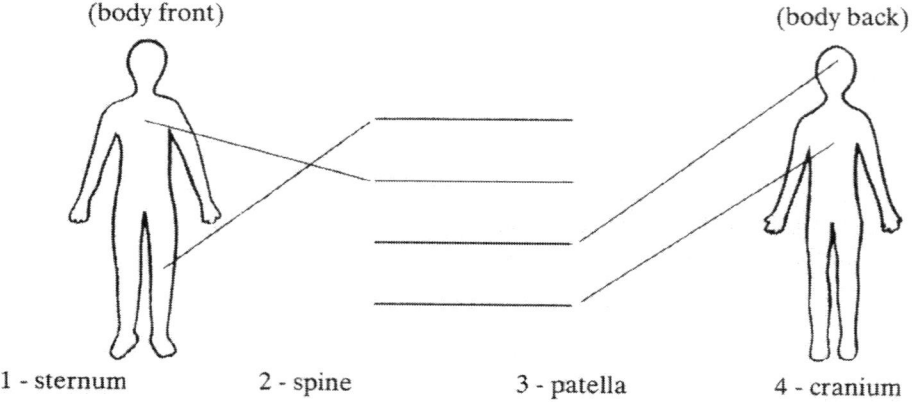

(body front)   (body back)

1 - sternum   2 - spine   3 - patella   4 - cranium

10.   Please give the definition of each of the following:

plié _____

au milieu _____

tendu _____

adage _____

battement frappé _____

allégro _____

rond de jambe _____

tour _____

développé _____

révérence _____

grand battement _____

ballet _____

Lesson Two

1. On another sheet of paper draw or trace the Positions Des Bras that your school uses and then attach it to this paper. Be sure to name each position.

2. Read the biography of Marie Taglioni and answer the following questions:

    a. The ballet _____ became Taglioni's signature role and awarded her the honorable nickname of _____ .

    b. Widely acclaimed for dancing on pointe, the romantic ballet showcased the _____ quality she brought to her roles.

3. A book was published in Paris by _____ in _____ upon which the foundation of ballet was based.

4. Louis XIV of France, referred to as the _____ , established an academy of dance in the year _____ which continues today known as the _____ .

5. Read the ballet "La Sylphide" and answer the following questions:

    a. "La Sylphide" was first presented in the year _____ with _____ as the sylph.

    b. The choreographer of the ballet was _____ .

6. Circle the names of characters found in this ballet from the list below:

    Colin   James   Effie   Clara   Gurn   Myrtha   Madge

7. What is the item that is fatal to the sylph? _____

8. a. Phalanges refer to _____ bones and _____ bones.

    b. Metatarsals are foot bones and tarsals are _____ bones.

9. Match the bone by writing the number on the line showing its location in the body.

(body front)   (body back)

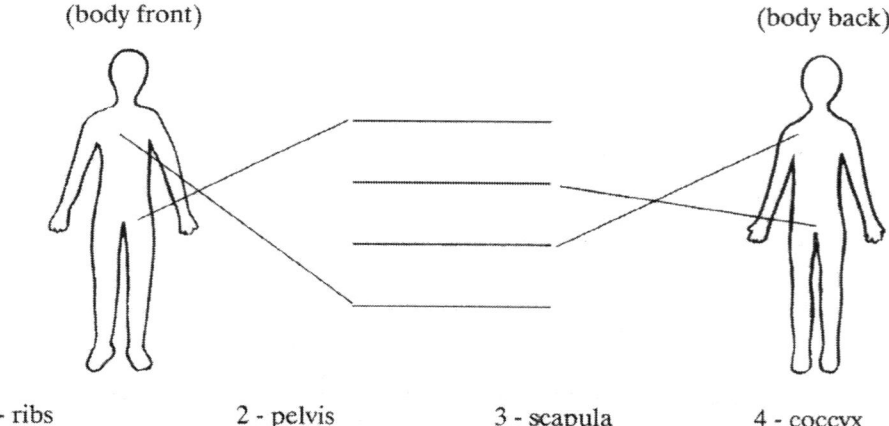

_____

_____

_____

_____

1 - ribs   2 - pelvis   3 - scapula   4 - coccyx

10. Please give the definition of each of the following:

à terre _____

en bas _____

pointe tendu _____

en haut _____

en l'air _____

plié _____

grand_____

frappé _____

demi_____

en dehors _____

en dedans _____

rond _____

Lesson Three

—⟨✦⟩—

1. In the space to the right draw a body or
stick figure. Then draw lines to indicate
the levels of the shoulders, ribs, hips (label
each) and the center line that divides the body
in half.

2. Read the biography of Carlotta Grisi and answer the questions below:

    a. _____ was the guiding force of Grisi's career and, although not
    always receiving credit, choreographed her role in the ballet _____.

    b. Grisi was one of the four ballerinas to appear on stage together for the first time in
    the ballet _____.

3. Name the father and son who were considered the greatest male dancers of the 18th
century. _____

4. Who shortened her skirt and removed the heels from her dancing shoes? _____

5. Then who loosened her skirt and bodice to gain freedom of expression? _____

6. Read the ballet "Giselle" and fill in the blanks below:

    a. First presented: _____.

    b. Who danced these roles?   Giselle _____
                                 Albrecht _____
                                 Myrtha _____

    c. All of the following characters are found in supporting roles in this ballet.
       (circle one)   True   or   False

        Hilarion   Wilfred   Berthe   Bathilde

7. The body's entire weight is supported by the _____.

8. Where is the cranium?_____ What is its common name? _____

9. Match the bone by writing the number on the line showing its location in the body.

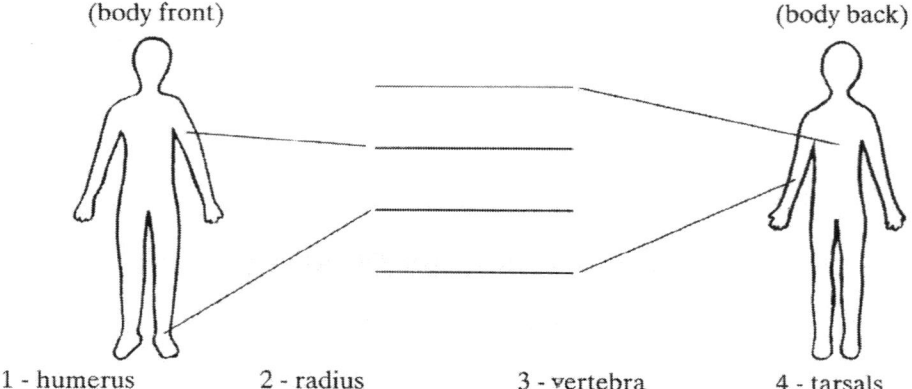

(body front)   (body back)

1 - humerus   2 - radius   3 - vertebra   4 - tarsals

10. Please give the definition of each of the following:

petit _____

bras bas _____

sur _____

élévation _____

barre_____

turn-out _____

au milieu _____

devant _____

révérence _____

derrière _____

corps de ballet _____

grand jeté_____

Lesson Four

1. From what part of the body does the turn-out come? _____

2. Dancers hold themselves in a long, tall and very erect posture that is achieved by
   what is called _____.

3. Read the biography of Marius Petipa and answer the questions below:

   a. In what year did Petipa become ballet master of the Imperial Theatre in
      St. Petersburg, Russia? _____

   b. Circle the ballets below which Petipa and the composer Tchaikovsky created
      together.

      Giselle   The Sleeping Beauty   Coppélia   The Nutcracker   Swan Lake

   c. Petipa's assistant choreographer was _____, and the two
      ballets for which he is most noted for his creativity with Petipa are:
      _____ and _____.

4. Whose theories led the way to the "ballet d'action"? _____

5. What was the technical innovation of the Romantic ballet period that was assured of
   its permanence by Marie Taglioni in the ballet "La Sylphide"? _____

6. Read the ballet "The Nutcracker" and fill in the blanks:

   a. First presented December 17, _____.

   b. This story is based on a tale by _____.

7. Match these scenes with their locations in "The Nutcracker".
   Snow Scene - _____
   Kingdom of Sweets - _____
   Christmas Party - _____

8. The Latin name for the thighbone is _____, and the Latin name for
   the tailbone is _____.

9.   Match the bone by writing the number on the line showing its location in the body.

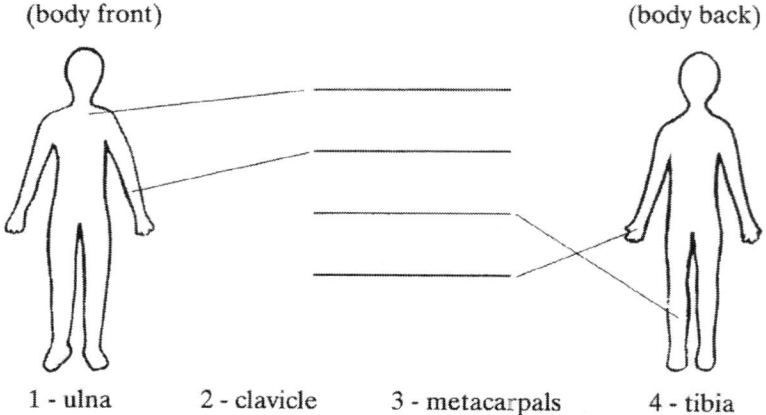

(body front)   (body back)

1 - ulna   2 - clavicle   3 - metacarpals   4 - tibia

10.   Please give the definition of each of the following:

écarté _____

retiré _____

dégagé _____

battement _____

rond de jambe _____

ballon _____

passé _____

temps levé _____

pas _____

jeté _____

développé _____

en _____

Lesson Five

1. A quality of a good corps de ballet is that each member is on the same angle while dancing on stage. To achieve this each dancer should: (check one)

    _____ a. Use their own square box mentally drawn around themselves.

    _____ b. Use the corners of the stage.

2. Read the biography of Jules Perrot and answer the following questions:

    a. Perrot choreographed the role of Giselle for _____.

    b. He is also the choreographer of _____, noteworthy as the first ballet which featured four of the leading ballerinas of the day in the same work.

3. Introduced by La Taglioni in "La Sylphide" was the costume which influenced and became traditional for the dancers of the period. What was it? _____

4. Considered the first ballerina from the United States, _____made her debut at the Paris Opéra in 1839.

5. Read the ballet "Pas de Quatre" and answer the questions below:

    a. Name the ballerinas for whom this ballet was choreographed. _____

    b. The dispute over the order of appearance in the solo positions was settled according to the _____ of the dancers.

6. How many bones are there in the lower leg? _____

7. How many bones are there in the lower arm? _____

8. How many ribs do we have? (circle one)   14 - 18 - 24 - 26

9.   Match the bone by writing the number on the line showing its location in the body.

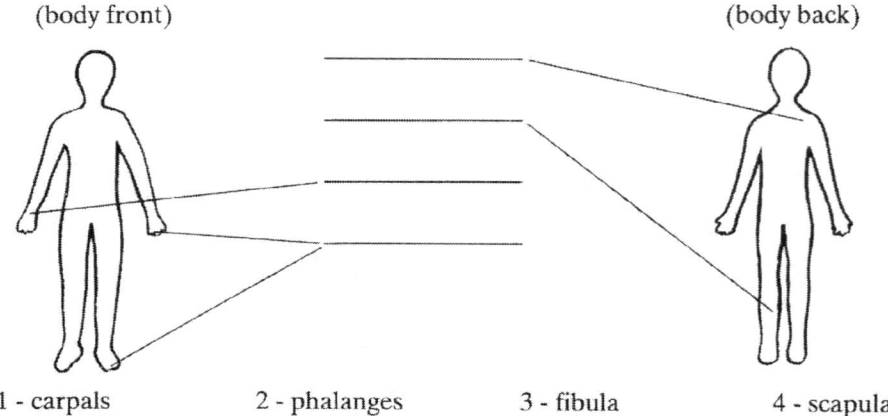

(body front)   (body back)

1 - carpals   2 - phalanges   3 - fibula   4 - scapula

10. Please give the definition of each of the following:

assemblé _____

glissade _____

soutenu _____

enchaînements _____

pas de bourrée _____

sans changer _____

chassé _____

croisé _____

sous-sus _____

choreography _____

pas de basque _____

grand jeté _____

Lesson Six

1. In the space below name (with English definitions) each of the basic positions of the body in the method that you are learning.

2. Read the biography of Arthur Saint-Léon and answer the questions below:

   a. Saint-Léon choreographed his most famous ballet _____ in 1870.

   b. His greatest contribution to ballet and his trademark was the use of

   _____.

3. The <u>Code of Terpsichore</u> which outlined a system of ballet technique was published in _____ by _____.

4. The Russian Imperial School was founded in _____.

5. Read the ballet "Coppélia" and answer the questions below:

   a. "Coppélia" is based on a story by _____.

   b. Write True or False beside these statements:

   1) Coppélia was a doll. _____
   2) Swanilda was a doll. _____
   3) Franz loved Swanilda. _____
   4) Dr. Coppélius was a toymaker. _____

6. The music for the ballet "Coppélia" was written by _____.

7. The bones in the wrist are called _____.

8.   The basin-like structure of the hipbone, or _____, forms a socket into
      which fits the largest bone in the body. The name of that bone is _____.

9.   Match the bone by writing the number on the line showing its location in the body.

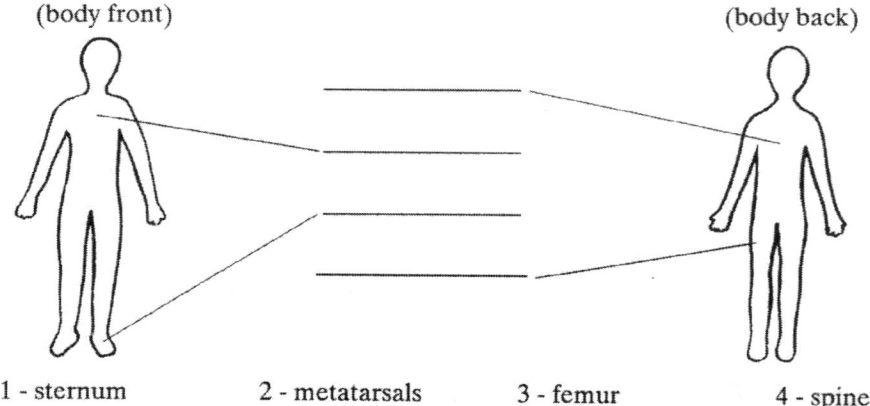

(body front)   (body back)

1 - sternum   2 - metatarsals   3 - femur   4 - spine

10.   Please give the definition of each of the following:

en croix _____

épaulé _____

de face _____

étendre _____

temps _____

extension _____

tutu _____

port de bras _____

effacé _____

posé _____

elancé _____

couru _____

Lesson Seven

1. Give a brief description of the three main schools of ballet technique.

   1._____
   _____

   2._____
   _____

   3._____
   _____

2. Read the biography of Fanny Cerito and answer the questions below:

   a. Cerito was married to the famous dancer/choreographer _____.

   b. One of the leading dancers of her time, Cerito appeared in
      _____ with Taglioni, Grisi and Grahn in _____ (date).

3. Name two of the most famous ballets created by Marius Petipa and composer Peter Ilych
   Tchaikovsky. _____ and _____

4. In 1801, _____ became choreographer at the Imperial Theatre and set out
   a syllabus for teaching. He is known as the _____ of Russian ballet.

5. Read the ballet "La Bayadère" and complete the following:

   a. First presented January 23, _____.

   b. Circle the names below of the characters found in this ballet:

      Solor   Myrtha   Nikia   Lissette   Gamsatti   Benno

6. In reference to "Kingdom of the Shades", what is another word for "shades"? _____

7. The backbone or spine has _____ curves and is made up of many bones called
   _____.

8.　　A patella is a _____.

9.　　Match the bone by writing the number on the line showing its location in the body.

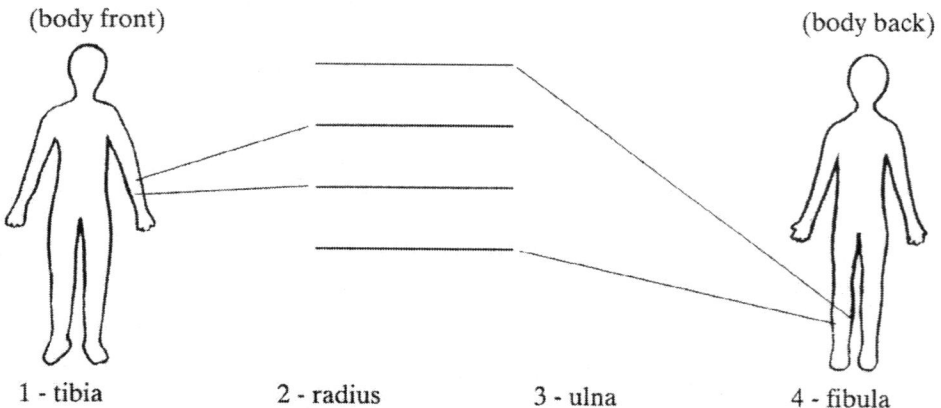

(body front)　　　　　　　　　　　　　　　　　　　　　(body back)

1 - tibia　　　　　2 - radius　　　　　3 - ulna　　　　　4 - fibula

10.　　Please give the definition of each of the following:

piqué _____

coupé _____

échappé _____

cou-de-pied _____

arabesque _____

pas de chat _____

allégro _____

en diagonale _____

adage _____

demi-contretemps _____

changement _____

en promenade _____

18.

Lesson Eight

1. In the space to the right, draw a rectangle and write the names found below in their proper places for stage directions.

   1. Downstage   2. Upstage   3. Center Stage   4. Stage Right
   5. Stage Left   6. Back Stage   7. Off Stage Wing Areas   8. Audience

2. Read the biography of Lucile Grahn and answer the questions below:

   a. Grahn was born in _____ in 1819, and became known as the _____ Taglioni.

   b. She was the youngest of the ballerinas who made history by appearing together in Perrot's ballet _____ in 1845.

   c. As a choreographer, Grahn created the "Bacchanale" for "Tannhauser" by _____.

3. The last Imperial prima ballerina assoluta was _____.

4. Read the ballet "The Sleeping Beauty" and complete the following:

   a. First presented _____.

   b. The story is from the fairy tale by _____.

   c. This is which of Tchaikovsky's ballet scores. (Circle one)
      First   Second   Third

5. The sleeping beauty's name is _____.

6. Enrico Cecchetti created roles in "The Sleeping Beauty" by performing in the Prologue and Act I as _____ , then dancing in Act III as the _____ in the now famous pas de deux by the same name.

7. The humerus is the _____ bone.

8. The stack of vertebrae form a canal which protects the _____ running through it.

9. Match the bone by writing the number on the line showing its location in the body.

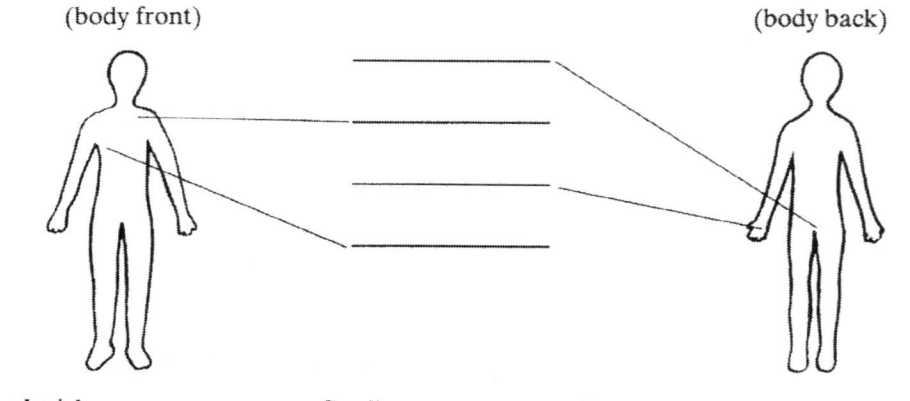

(body front)   (body back)

1 - clavicle   2 - ribs   3 - coccyx   4 - metacarpals

10. Please give the definition of each of the following:

soubresaut _____

fondu _____

en arrière _____

pas de deux _____

en avant _____

premier danseur _____

balancé _____

fermé _____

ballerina _____

temps lié _____

ballet _____

chaînés _____

Lesson Nine

1. Name three characteristics of a dancer's stance.

   1. _____ 2. _____ 3. _____

2. Name the ballet movement/position described below in sports terms:

   a. A football player kicks the ball through the goal posts using a _____.

   b. A baseball batter stands with knees bent, legs apart and if turned out would
      be in _____.

3. Read the biography of Mathilde Kschessinska and answer the following questions:

   a. Kschessinska entered the Imperial Ballet School in _____
      and made her debut at the Maryinsky in _____.

   b. World politics would play a major role in her life, but in 1895 she was granted
      the status of _____.

4. Complete the following list of ballet masters at the Imperial Theatre beginning in 1801 with
      Charles-Louis Didelot:

           1848 to 1858 - _____
           1859 to 1870 - _____
           1870 to 1903 - _____

5. Read the ballet "Swan Lake" and answer the questions below:

   a. This ballet is noted for the dual roles named_____ and _____.

   b. The lake was made from the Swan Queen's mother's _____.

6. The Ivanov/Petipa version was first presented at the Maryinsky Theatre on _____.

7. Some of the ribs in front are connected to the _____, or _____.

8.   The shoulder girdle is made up of the collarbones and shoulder blades. What is the Latin name of each of these? The _____ and the _____.

9.   Match the bone by writing the number on the line showing its location in the body.

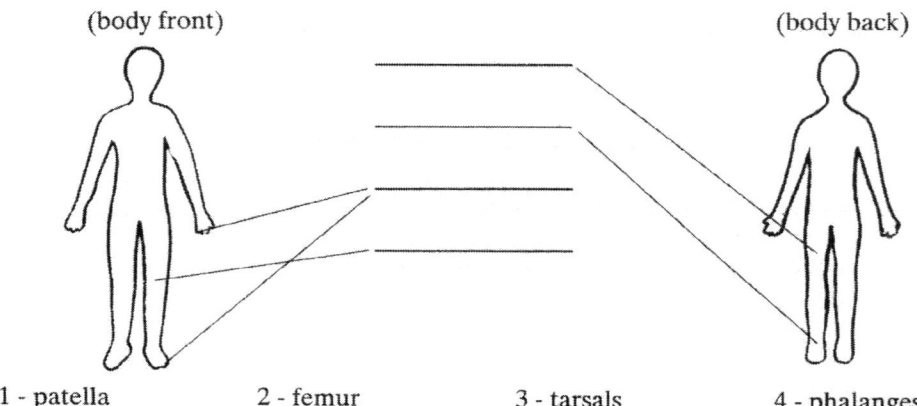

(body front)   (body back)

1 - patella   2 - femur   3 - tarsals   4 - phalanges

10.   Please give the definition of each of the following:

variation _____

relevé _____

bras _____

sauté _____

fouetté _____

à la seconde _____

choreography _____

attitude _____

préparation _____

Terpsichore _____

quatrième _____

pirouette _____

The Ballet Book

Theory

A Dancer's Stance

The stance of a dancer is unmistakable to see and feel. It is one of elegance and suggests pride and noble bearing. It is one of the very first things taught at ballet schools and is used throughout a dancer's career, and on into their everyday lives as well.

Turn-Out

The first thing that is seen to be different from the way most people stand is that a dancer's feet are turned to the sides. This is called turn-out and its purpose is to enable the dancer to move, using the steps of ballet, as smoothly and quickly in any direction as possible. The turn-out is achieved by using the muscles to rotate the legs from inside the hip sockets. To turn out only from the knees or ankles could result in injuries. Development of a correct turn-out takes a long time and very careful exercises.

Pull-Up

The next thing that sets dancers apart from most people is a long, tall and very erect posture achieved by what is called pull-up. This, too, takes a long time and careful practice to make it work. The most common mistake made trying to pull up is that of sticking the rib cage forward, causing the back to arch. A good way to think about pulling up is to remember that the shoulders should be right over the ribs and the ribs and shoulders should be right over the hips, with the stomach being lifted up and back into the spine. Holding the body in this straight position, lift yourself up through the backbone while thinking about trying to touch the ceiling with the top of the head. If your teacher says to lift your chin higher, remember, it's only the chin that's up and not the ribs thrust out, too.

Placement

To help you understand correct placement, stand in front of a mirror and imagine a line drawn from left to right across the top of your shoulders. Now draw another line through your ribs and another through your hips for a total of three horizontal lines. These three lines should have the same amount of space between them on each side. If one space seems like the lines are closer together than the same space on the other side, check yourself. Perhaps a shoulder is dropped, or one side of the rib cage is collapsed, or a hip is lifted. These things tend to spoil the "look" of the classical line of the body. They can also affect your balance and the ability to control movement for the proper execution of a step or series of steps. (See Figures 1 & 2) Another line to help your placement in port de bras is to imagine a straight line from your head to your feet down the center of your body. This will separate the right side and left side. When you present your port de bras, one arm should not cross over that center line into the other arm's side. (See Figure 3)

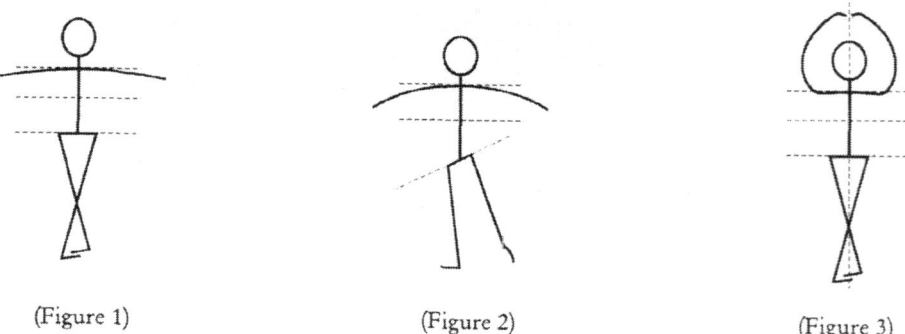

24.   (Figure 1)   (Figure 2)   (Figure 3)

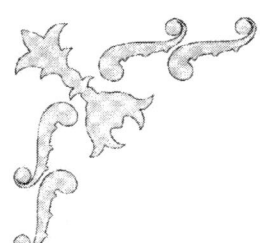

The Three Main Schools Of Technique

Although there are several schools of ballet technique used throughout the world, they all evolved from the Italian, French and Russian styles, or a combination thereof. These three main schools each teach a good foundation for dance students. The differences are mainly in the styles and approaches. One should not be considered better than the others, as each is equally valid.

Italian (Cecchetti)

This school of technique is known for its clean, classical lines and the development of virtuosity within a delicate framework.

French

This school of technique is known for its soft, graceful movements, with a little ornate, rococo feeling in its style.

Russian

This school of technique is known for its strength in spacious lines and movements of a grand, flamboyant, and rich style.

Fixed Points For The Dancer

A classical line of the body is the goal to which all dancers aspire. While practicing in the class the teacher will correct you and you will be able to see it in the mirror. But you must also memorize what it "feels" like in order to hit that position again, any and every time you need it.

Here is an exercise that will help. Visualize yourself in the middle of a square box that you've drawn around yourself. Each flat line of that box around you, and each corner of that box, is a marker for you. It really doesn't matter all that much whether you number them or use the alphabet to label them, as long as **you** know where they are and can center your body to that point in order to make the desired position the clean line it is supposed to be.

The diagrams below illustrate two versions of the box.

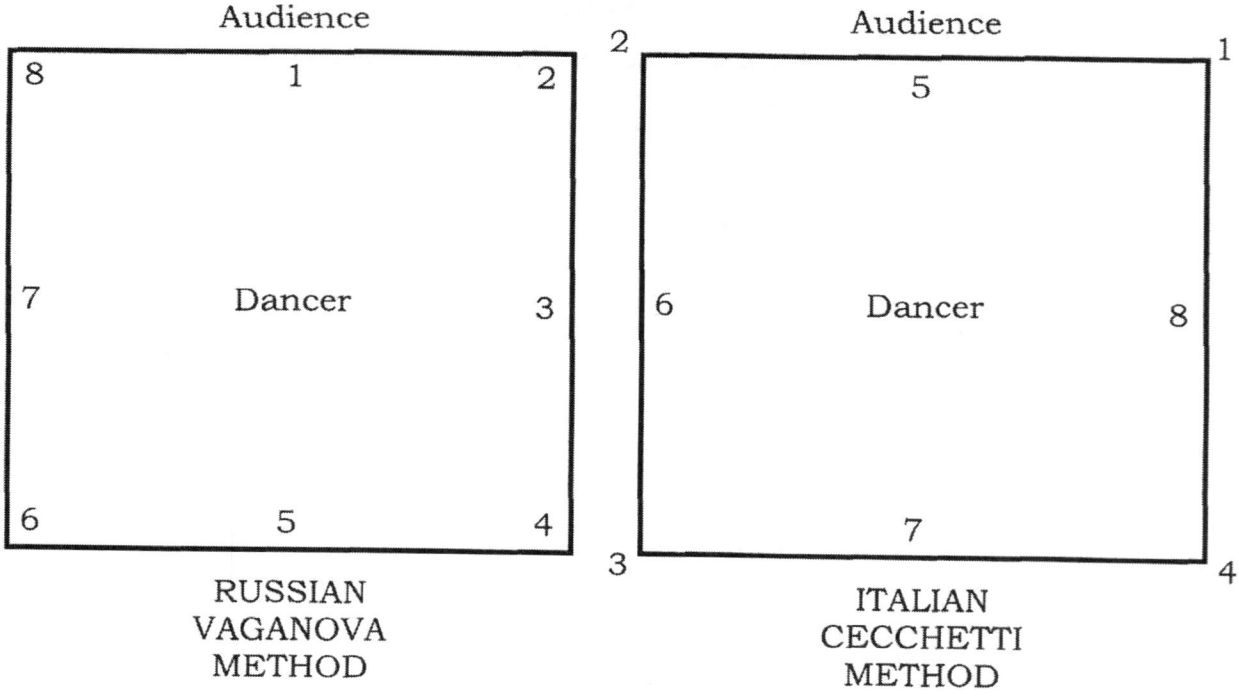

RUSSIAN
VAGANOVA
METHOD

ITALIAN
CECCHETTI
METHOD

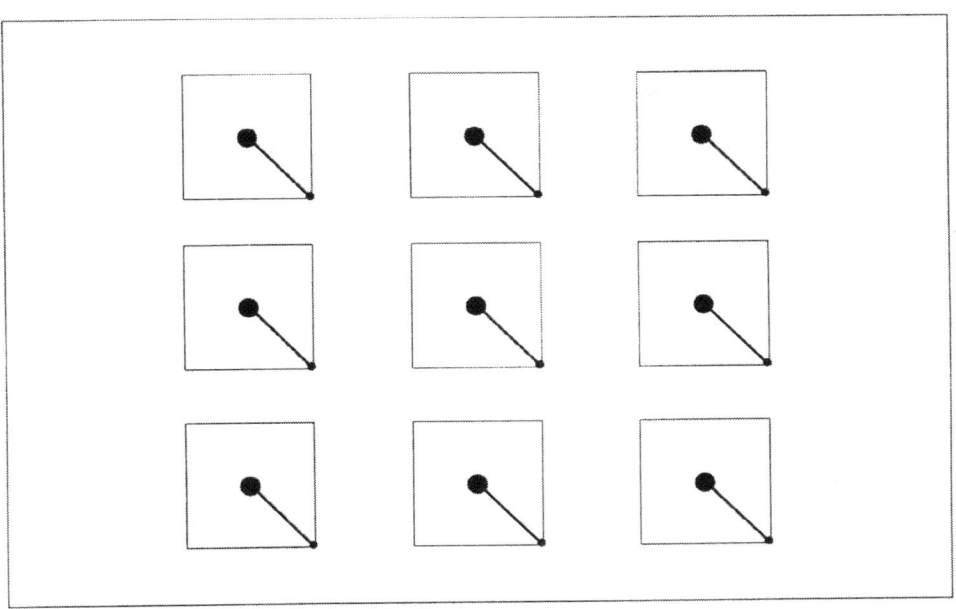

Audience

Now to illustrate the use of both stage directions and the dancer's square box properly, look at these diagrams. The top diagram shows all the dancers on stage in uniform positions toward their own corner. This is a very good look for a corps de ballet. The diagram below shows the dancers facing the downstage left corner of the stage (by the way, a stage is usually more rectangular than square in shape). This is not necessarily a good look for a corps de ballet, as everyone is on a different angle.

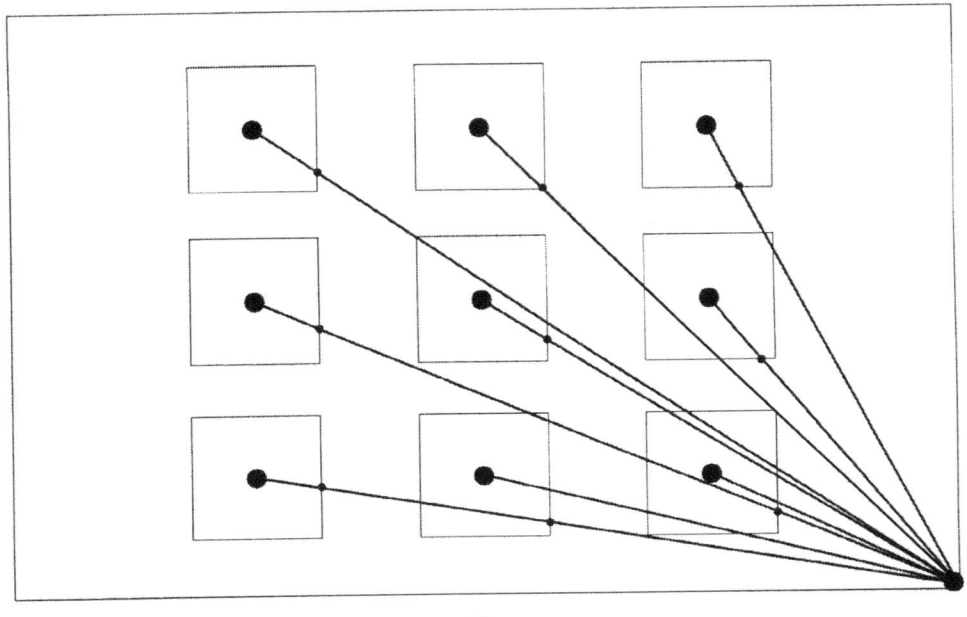

Audience

Stage Directions

The terms used for stage directions come from a period in the theatre when the stage was raked, or tilted down, toward the audience for better viewing by the audience. That meant that the footlights were literally **down** at the foot of the stage. To move to the back of the stage meant "climbing" **up** the incline to the top part of the stage. Although footlights and raked stages are not used as often today, the terminology has remained. The directions stage left and stage right mean to **your** left or right as you face the audience. The diagram below illustrates the standard stage directions.

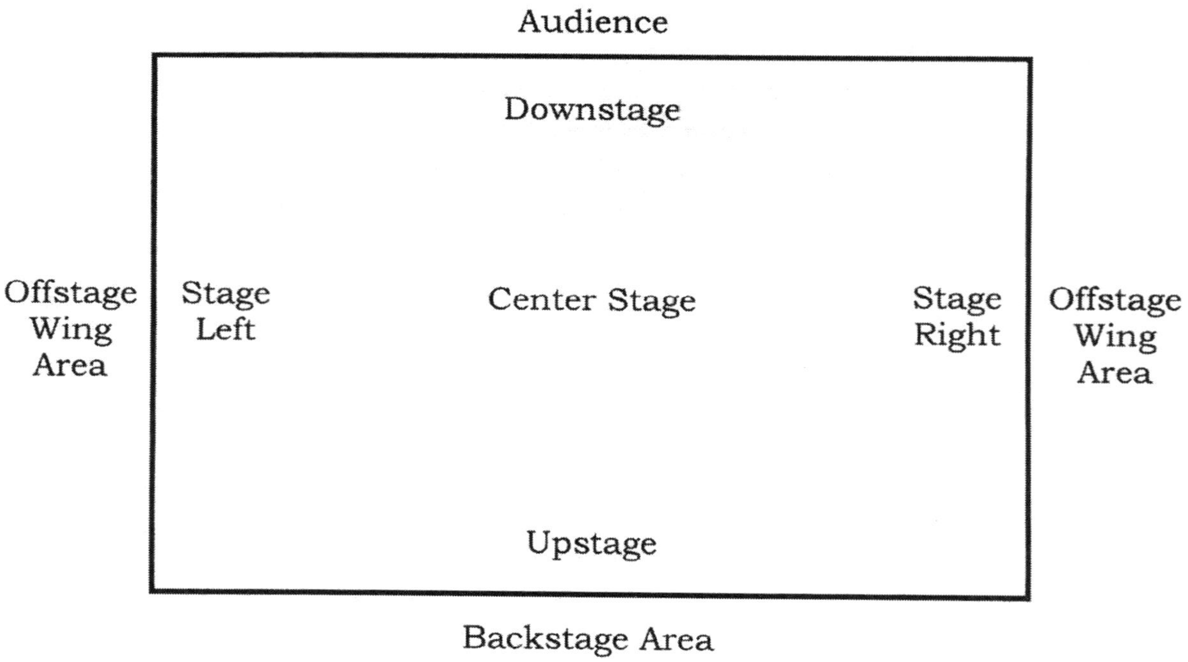

Audience

	Downstage	
Offstage Wing Area	Stage Left Center Stage Stage Right	Offstage Wing Area
	Upstage	

Backstage Area

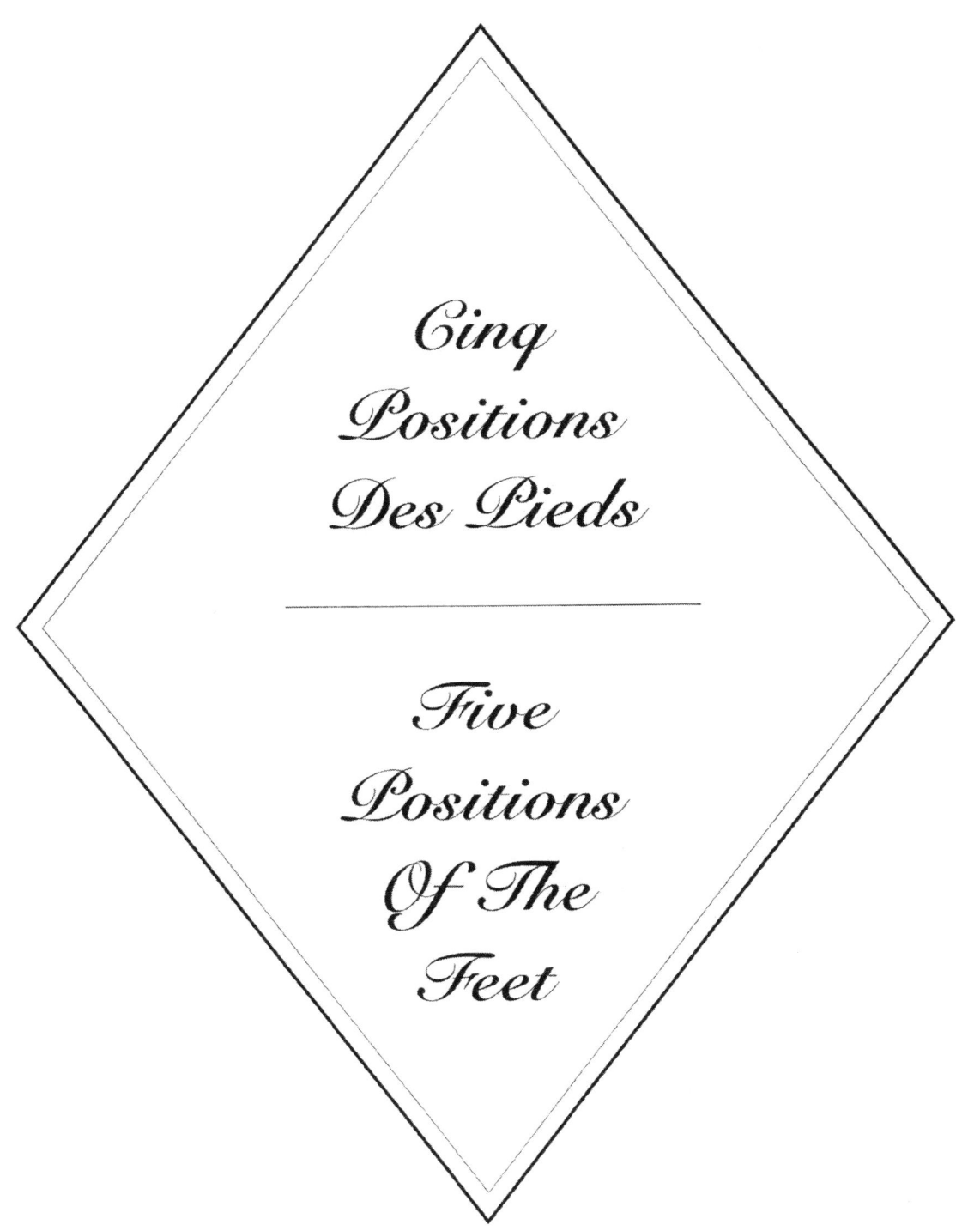

Cinq

Positions

Des Pieds

Five

Positions

Of The

Feet

Positions of the Feet

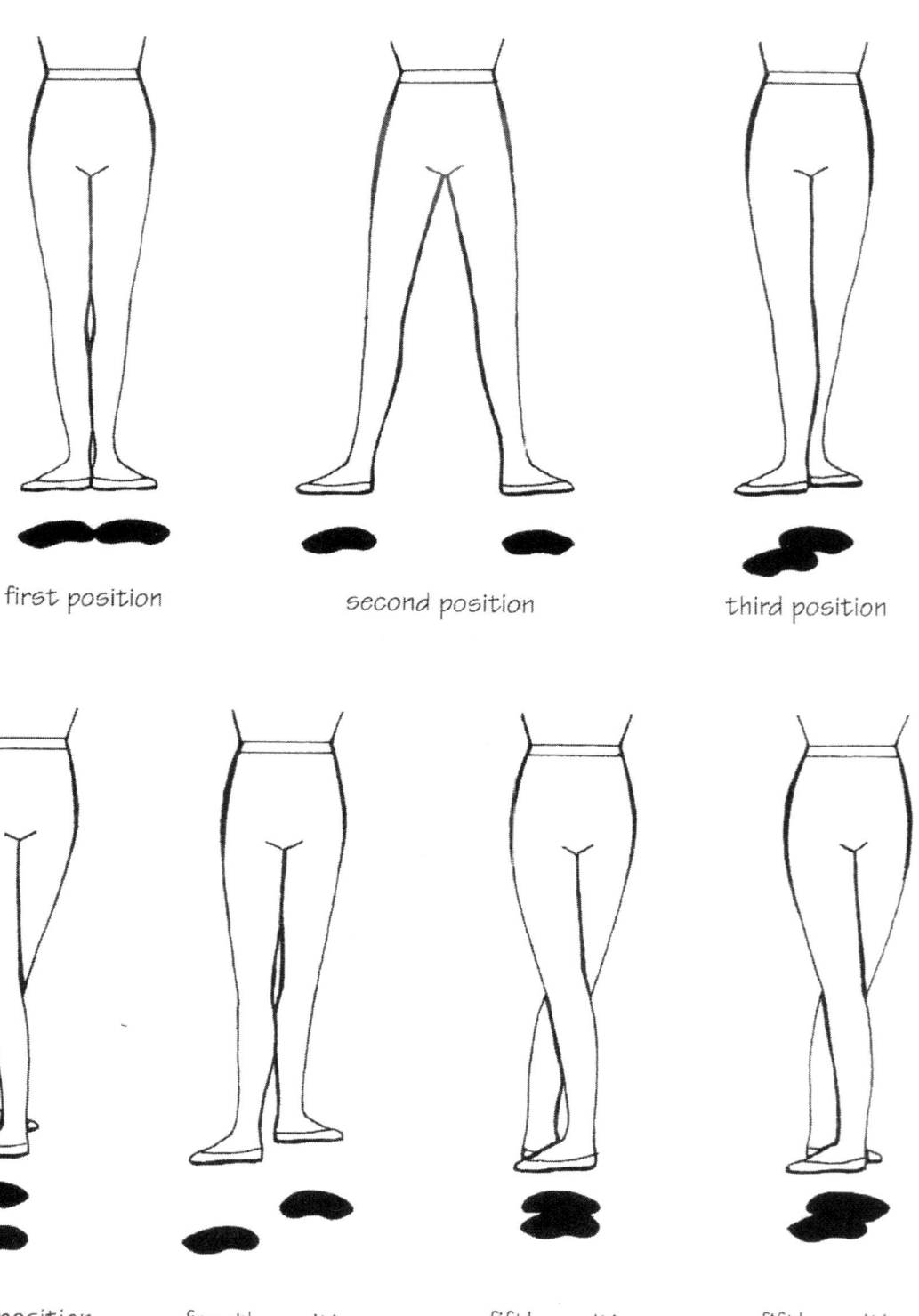

first position

second position

third position

fourth position
croisé

fourth position
ouvert

fifth position
(Russian/French)
(completely toe-to-heel)

fifth position
(Cecchetti)

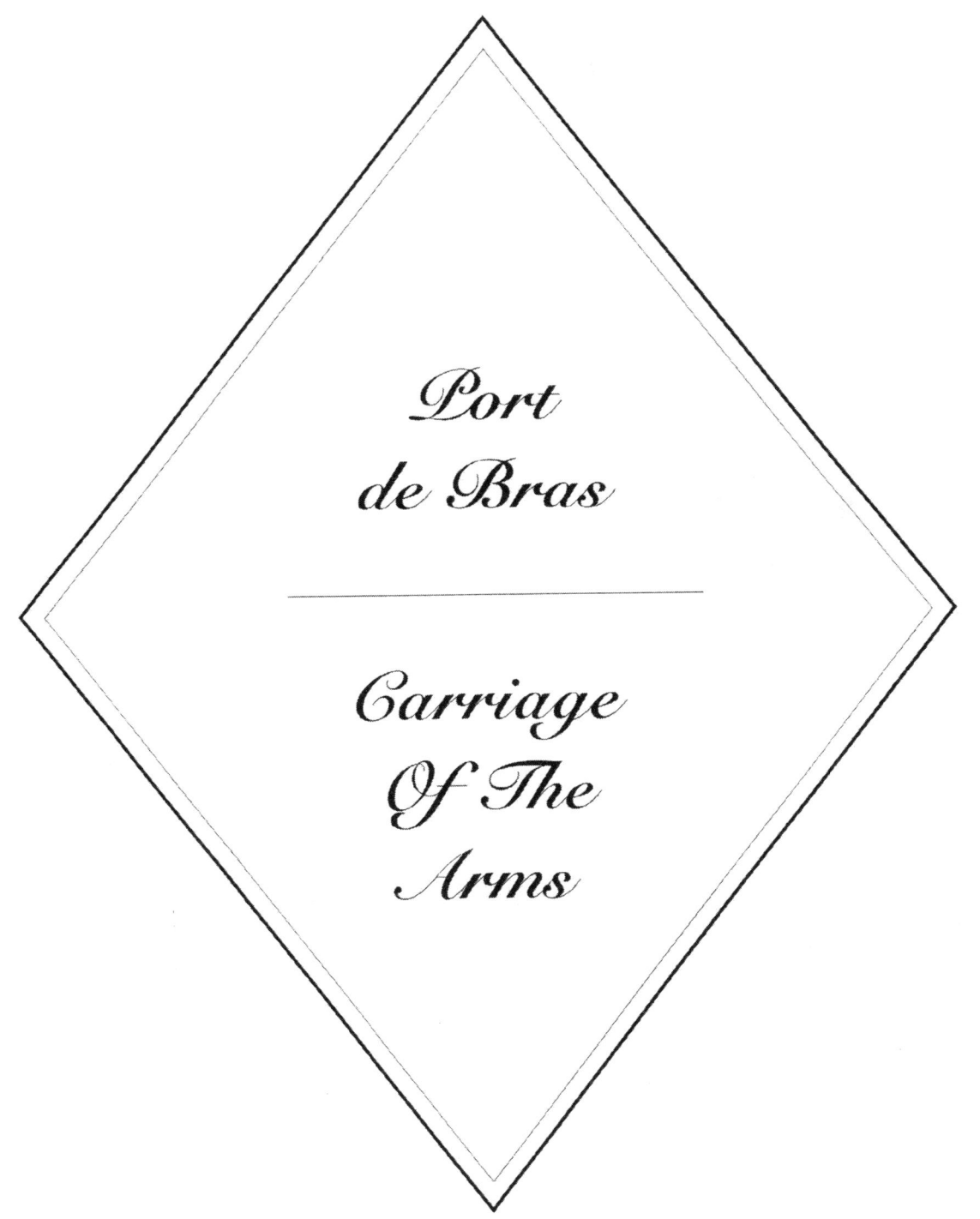

Port
de Bras

_____

Carriage
Of The
Arms

Port de Bras - Cecchetti

1st position
(feet - 1st position)

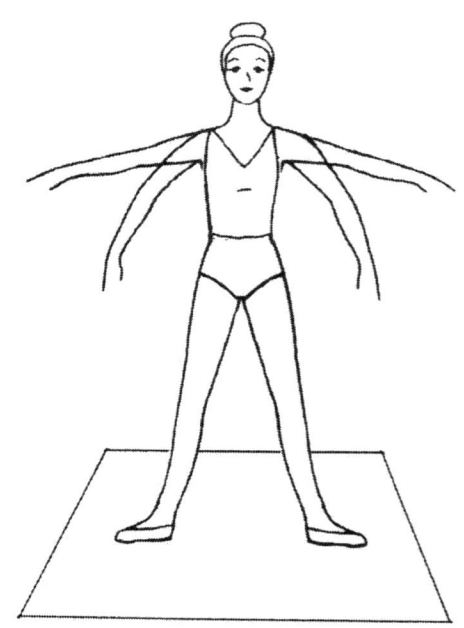

2nd & demi 2nd position
(feet - 2nd position)

3rd position
(feet - 3rd position)

4th position en avant
(feet - 4th position croisé)

Port de Bras - Cecchetti

4th position en haut
(feet - 4th position croisé)

5th position en bas
(feet - 5th position)

5th position en avant
(feet - 5th position)

5th position en haut
(feet - 5th position)

Port de Bras - French

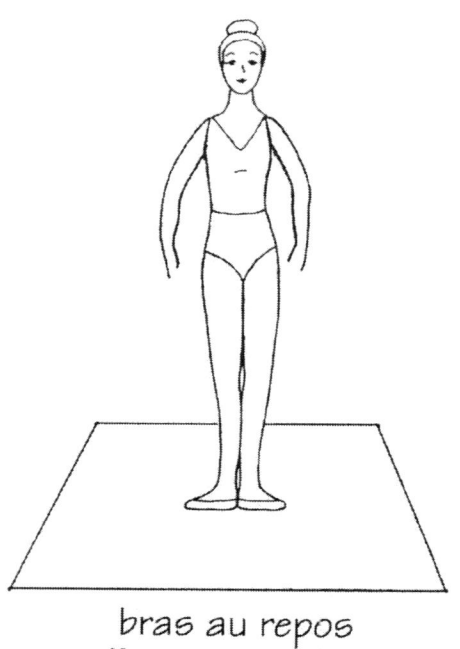

bras au repos
(feet - 1st position)

1st position
(feet - 1st position)

2nd position
(feet - 2nd position)

Port de Bras - French

3rd position
(feet - 3rd position)

4th position
(feet - 4th position)

5th position
(feet - 5th position)

Port de Bras - Russian
(Feet Are All In 1st Position)

preparatory

1st position

2nd position

3rd position

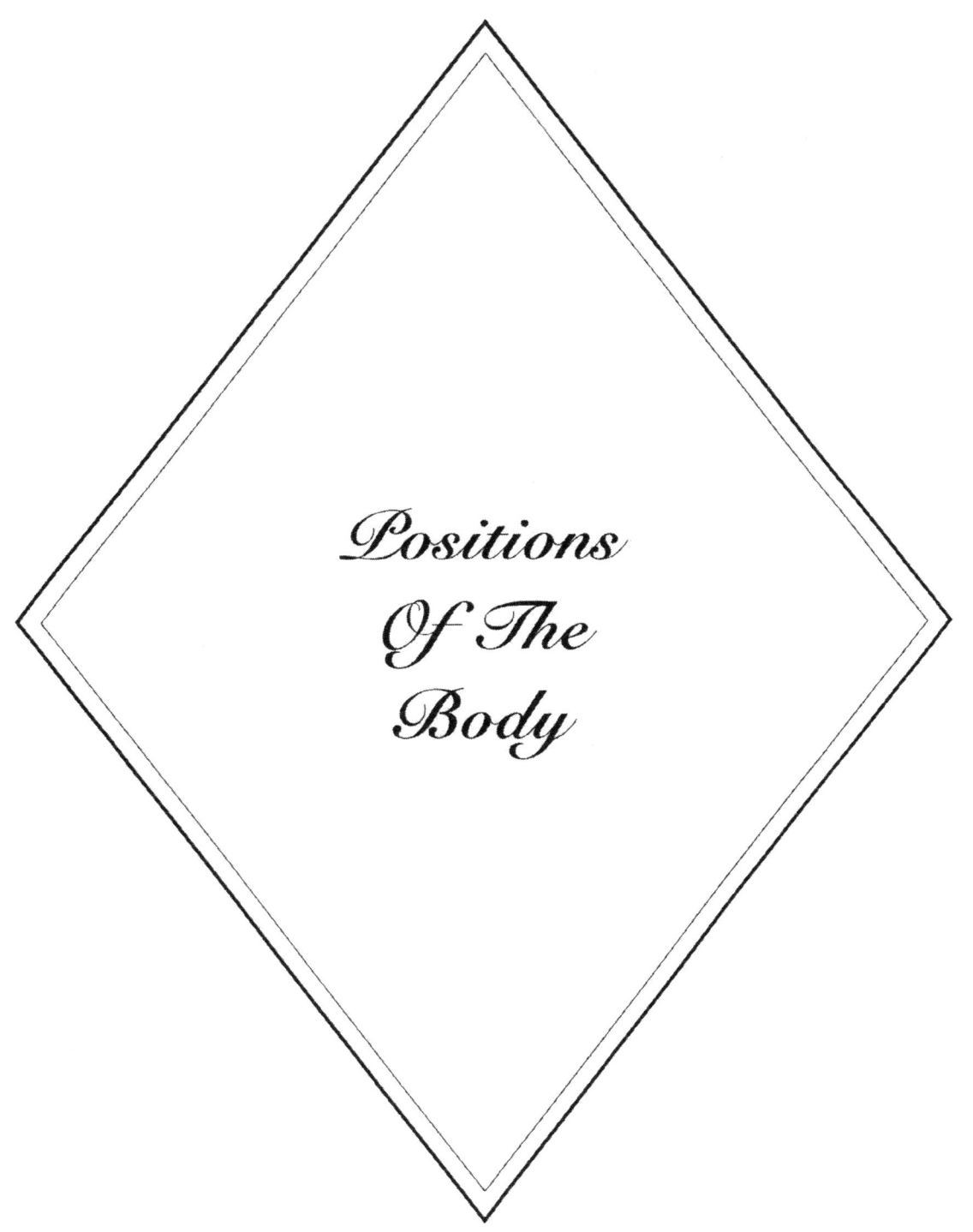

Positions
Of The
Body

Body Positions - Cecchetti

croisé devant

à la quatrième devant

écarté

effacé

Body Positions - Cecchetti

à la seconde

épaulé

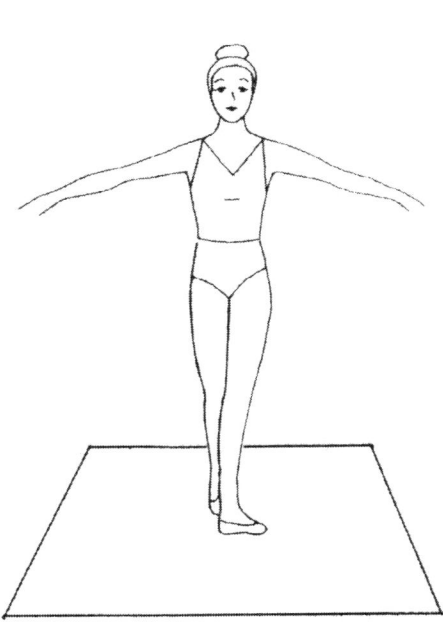

à la quatrième derrière

croisé derrière

Body Positions - Russian/French

croisé devant

croisé derrière

à la quatrième devant

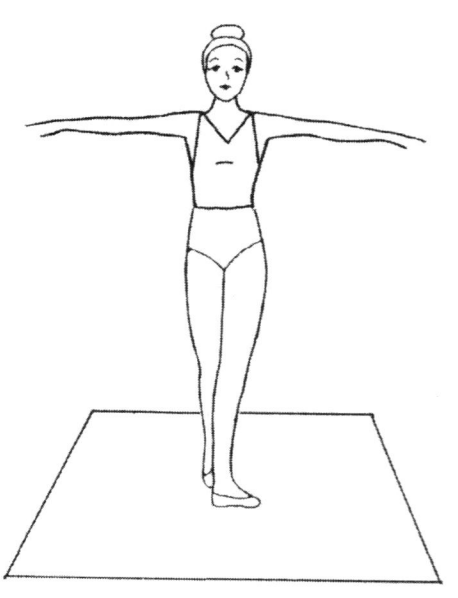

à la quatrième derrière

Body Positions - Russian/French

à la seconde

écarte devant

écarté derrière

41.

Body Positions - Russian/French

efface devant

efface derrière

épaulé devant

épaulé derrière

The Dancer's Clothes

Jerkin

The jerkin was an outer garment worn by men in the 16th and 17th centuries . . . a short coat or vest, tightly fitted and waist-length. When sleeveless, the jerkin was worn over a shirt with long, loose sleeves. Sometimes the jerkin was made of leather with sleeves of a heavy, rich fabric.

Leotard

Named for Jules Leotard, the 19th century trapeze artist who devised it, the leotard remains relatively unchanged today . . . a one-piece body stocking designed for both comfort and freedom of movement.

Tights

Tights as we know them can be traced back to the Middle Ages when knitted or cloth hose were worn to cover the foot and part of the leg. These short hose grew longer during the 14th and 15th centuries. In the 16th century they finally became full-length tights, although they were still worn as two separate garments. Upper hose would be like our modern underpants and lower hose were more like stockings. Over the centuries, better machines for knitting and innovative materials (like lycra) have created the smooth, well-fitting and comfortable tights we know today.

Tutu

The focal point of the ballerina's costume, today's tutu has evolved from the early dancer's heavy floor-length dress. In earlier centuries it was considered indecent for a woman to show any part of her leg; it was scandalous in the early 1700s when Marie Carmago shortened her skirt to calf-length.

As times changed, the tutu got shorter to allow more mobility and for the audience to see the dancer's legs as she danced. Today's ballerinas still wear the long, romantic tutu, the mid-calf length. In street fashion it became known as the "ballerina-length" dress. Female dancers often appear in the short, classical "pancake" tutu worn with or without a decorative overskirt. A third length tutu is also worn in some ballets. Approximately knee-length, it is between the lengths of the classical and romantic tutus.

No one knows for certain where the term "tutu" came from. Here are three possibilities:
1. From the word "tunique" (tunic),
2. From "tulle", the sheer fabric used in the costume, and
3. A French slang word for "baby's bottom", referring to the rows of tiny ruffles on the costume.

How To Enjoy A Ballet

Going to see a ballet can be frightening for some people. It helps to know what to expect. Like going to a ball game, you enjoy it so much more when you know the rules and can follow along. For example, if you know the name of the ballet you will be seeing, you can then determine which one of the three styles it will be:

Story Ballet

The plot of the story unfolds and we see what
happens to the characters

Mood Ballet

Creates a mood - no story is used

Abstract Ballet

Music provides the plot - one group of dancers represent
the melody, another group moves only to
counter-rhythm or drums, flutes, violins, etc.

Reading the story of the ballet before you will be seeing it always helps you to follow along.

Remember that every performance is different because dancers are human with the capacity to make mistakes. Seeing several ballets several times helps to train the eye for the little things that can make an evening at the ballet much more exciting.

Ballets are theatrical productions that use several other art forms in its presentation such as music, stage design, lighting, costume design, etc.

Understanding some of the technical difficulties of the technique helps intensify your appreciation of it. For instance, when we watch the Olympics, we start to learn a bit about the different events and what to watch for in their presentations. It doesn't mean we have to know all of it; the understanding makes us better appreciate the event and the efforts being put forth by the athletes.

However, unlike sporting events, ballet is an art and should be watched and enjoyed with the heart and emotions as well as the intellect.

The Ballet Book

Biographies

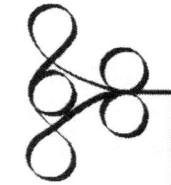

Fanny Elssler
(1810-1884)
"The Pagan"

Born in Vienna, Austria, in 1810, Fanny Elssler came from a family of professional musicians. As the Elsslers were not well off, each of the five children were encouraged to become self-supporting as soon as possible. Fanny, age 7, and her sister Thérèse, 9, were enrolled in the ballet school of the Kaernthertor Theatre in Vienna where they quickly showed great promise. Under the guidance of Jean Aumer, ballet master until Elssler was 11, and later under Philippe Taglioni, Elssler's talent and musicality matured. She made her debut in 1822.

In 1824 Elssler went to the San Carlo Opera in Naples and then, in 1830, accepted a contract with the Berlin Opera to appear with her sister, Thérèse, as leading dancers.

Much has been written about the rivalry between Fanny Elssler and Marie Taglioni, the reigning ballerina of that time. Appearing at the King's Theatre in London in 1833, Elssler was coolly received at first. Her style was very different; where Taglioni was fragile and ethereal, Elssler was earthy and sensual, a "pagan dancer" as noted by the poet Théophile Gautier. Elssler was quite lovely, had an exciting staccato style and frequently incorporated Spanish folk dances into the ballet. Her specialty became colorful character dances, most notably "La Cachucha", which became her signature dance.

Elssler was engaged for the Paris Opéra by Dr. Véron, the Opéra's director in 1834. Sensing good box office results, Véron fanned the flames of the supposed rivalry between Elssler and Taglioni. Audiences swarmed to the theatre; Paris was as divided on its "favorites" as England had been. Unfortunately for Dr. Véron, his scheming backfired and both ballerinas left Paris. Taglioni journeyed to Russia where she stayed for three years.

Being more adventurous at heart, Elssler accepted an offer to go to America in 1840. She appeared in almost every major American city and was widely acclaimed. It was a lucrative trip, so lucrative that she ignored her contract with the Paris Opéra and extended her stay; what had started out as a three-month tour stretched into two years.

When she returned to Europe, Paris was closed to her. She continued dancing, appearing again in Berlin, Vienna and London, and then making a three-year tour of Italy. In 1848 she went to St. Petersburg where, although past her prime, she excited audiences with her beauty and talent. She made her last appearance on stage with a performance of "Foust" in Vienna in 1851.

Elssler retired in her native Vienna and lived in some comfort because of the fortune she brought back with her from America and Russia. She died in November, 1884.

Elssler was mourned by the world for she had brought an earthiness and sensuality to the cool, distant persona of ballet's Romantic period.

Marie Taglioni

(1804-1884)
"The Sylph"

Born in Stockholm, Sweden, in 1804, Marie Taglioni began her dance training at the age of 12 in Paris. She was an uninspired student and, after five years, was not ready to debut. Philippe Taglioni, her father and himself a noted dancer, choreographer and ballet master, took over her training. After six months of intensive training, Taglioni made her debut in Vienna in 1822.

"La Sylphide", which became Taglioni's signature role, premiered in 1832 in Paris. In this ballet she received wide acclaim for her ethereal grace and dancing on pointe. Her costume, the long, filmy, white tutu, remains a romantic ballet tradition. The sylphide look became the rage - dresses, hairstyles, flowers and "sylphide" attitudes were adopted by fashionable ladies.

Now heralded as "La Taglioni", Marie married Alfred, Comte Gilbert de Voisins in 1834. Two months of marriage ended when he left her, and ten years later he obtained a legal separation.

Shortly after her husband deserted her, Taglioni was pressed into a highly publicized rivalry with Fanny Elssler, another leading ballerina of the Paris Opéra Ballet. She left Paris in 1837 and went to the Imperial Theatre in St. Petersburg, Russia, where the Tsar himself showered her with jewels. In 1840 she returned to western Europe, dancing in Vienna and London.

Another production for which Taglioni is known was the famous premiere of the "Pas de Quatre" - a ballet created to showcase four of the foremost ballerinas of the era - Taglioni, Fanny Cerrito, Lucile Grahn and Carlotta Grisi.

Marie Taglioni retired in 1847 after a glittering career. In 1858 she returned to Paris to teach advanced classes at the Paris Opéra Ballet. The Franco-Prussian War caused her to move in 1870 to London where she began her own school. Ten years later Taglioni moved back to France to live with her son and, in 1884, she died at the age of 80.

Taglioni is still considered to be possibly the greatest ballerina of the romantic era. The romantic ballet perfectly showcased the ethereal quality she brought to her roles. Her technique and elevation contributed to her renowned airy grace.

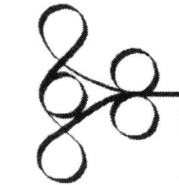

Carlotta Grisi

(1819-1899)
"The First Giselle"

Carlotta Grisi began her ballet training at the Conservatory of Music in Milan at the age of 7, and by the time she was 10 had become a member of the corps de ballet at La Scala.

On a tour of Italy in 1833 she met the man who would be the guiding force of her career. Jules Perrot, the French dancer who would later receive great fame as a choreographer, was immediately attracted to the young Italian ballerina. He became Grisi's teacher and partner; his desire was that her career should eclipse those of Taglioni and Elssler. To that end, they danced together all over Europe.

In February of 1841 Grisi made her debut at the Paris Opéra in Donizetti's opera, "La Favorite", partnered by Lucien Petipa. However, it was in the same year that she would appear in what would become her greatest role. The ballet "Giselle" was created by a group of the most talented writers, musicians, scenic designers and choreographers of the era. Grisi would dance the title role written for her, partnered again by Petipa. Although he received no credit for so doing, Perrot actually choreographed the role of Giselle for Grisi.

"Giselle" was extraordinarily successful. In 1842 Grisi danced the role in England. She also created the leading role in "La Jolie Fille de Grand" that year. Having become a favorite in England, Grisi returned each year for the next nine years. Perrot had by this time devoted himself to choreography and Grisi was the star in most of his creations. In 1843 she danced "La Péri", in 1844 she created the leading role in "La Esmeralda" and in 1845 made her famous appearance with Taglioni, Cerito and Grahn in "Pas de Quatre".

With the end of the Romantic era looming, Perrot settled in Russia. When Grisi arrived in St. Petersburg in 1851, they became onstage partners again and danced for another three years.

In 1854 Grisi retired at the height of her career and settled in Paris. By the time she died in 1899 at the age of 79, the ballet world she had known had all but disappeared.

Although her death went practically unnoticed, Grisi was and still is remembered by the ballet world for creating the title role in "Giselle", perhaps the most exacting test of a ballerina's talents even today.

Marius Petipa

(1819-1910)
"The Master"

French by birth, Marius Petipa was first a dancer and choreographer, but it was as ballet master of the Imperial Theatre in St. Petersburg, Russia, that he made his undeniable contributions to the art of ballet.

He received his training from his father, Jean, and danced throughout Europe until 1847. At that time Jean Petipa was appointed ballet master of the Imperial Theatre and Marius went to Russia with him as his assistant and soloist. When Jean's contract expired, however, Marius remained with the Imperial Ballet. He began teaching in 1854 and by the next year was head of the school. It was only after he was appointed ballet master in 1870 that he was able to combine his vast knowledge and experience into a lasting legacy. During his career Petipa created over 50 ballets, revived 17 others and arranged dances for 34 operas.

The number is impressive but audiences were losing interest because, in many cases, the limited plot became lost in too many dances that had little or nothing to do with the story. As a "last chance" the Director of the Imperial Theatres orchestrated a collaboration of Petipa and the composer Peter Ilyich Tchaikovsky to create a ballet around the fairy tale "The Sleeping Beauty". Petipa's vast knowledge of every aspect of ballet went into the creation of the ballet ... not just the story with choreography, but elaborate production notes, suggestions as to props, set design and costuming and such extensive musical instruction that it enabled Tchaikovsky

to write what he himself called "some of my best music". "The Sleeping Beauty" was such a success that it was decided that Petipa and Tchaikovsky should create a ballet from "Tales of a Nutcracker" by E.T.A. Hoffmann.

It is impossible to mention "Nutcracker" without understanding the input from another highly gifted choreographer, Lev Ivanov. Petipa's assistant, Ivanov had to take over the choreography for "Nutcracker" when Petipa became ill. His way of working was different than Petipa's ... Ivanov let the music help create his dances while Petipa set the dances based on his musical instructions. Ivanov was confined to working within Petipa's extensive and detailed notes, and the ballet as a whole was not successful.

Ivanov's greatest creative work is considered to be two acts of "Swan Lake", an earlier and unsuccessful ballet by Tchaikovsky. Reworked by Petipa and Ivanov after the death of the composer, "Swan Lake" became quite successful even with its two distinctively different styles of choreography. Ivanov never achieved the fame of Petipa, but his creativity and contributions to these classic ballets are every bit as important as "the master's".

Marius Petipa retired in 1903 and died in 1910. His detailed notes for story, music and production have been preserved, creating a continuity through the generations. He left the legacy of three classics, "The Sleeping Beauty" and, with Ivanov, "The Nutcracker" and "Swan Lake".

Jules Joseph Perrot
(1810-1892)
"The Actor"

Born in France in 1810, Perrot began his career as dancer/choreographer by performing throughout the provinces as a circus clown and pantomimist. It is very possible that this earliest experience was what gave Perrot his distinctive touch in both dancing and choreography, that of adding true acting.

While still a teenager Perrot began studying classical ballet with Auguste Vestris and made his debut with the Paris Opéra in 1830. It is said that Perrot was homely to look at and, because of this, Vestris encouraged him to move about quickly so the audience would not be able to get a good look at him. Happily, this advice was well taken and Perrot became noted for his speed, turns and leaps. He became known as one of the great male dancers of all time, certainly in an era that was noted for and dominated by the great Romantic ballerinas. One of these ballerinas, Marie Taglioni, was so jealous of his success that she refused to appear with him, forcing him to leave the Paris Opéra in 1835.

Perrot toured throughout Europe, dancing his own ballets which included "Caterina", "Esmeralda" and "Faust", frequently partnering Carlotta Grisi, whom he had met in 1833. They returned to the Paris Opéra in 1841 where they received a warm welcome, but Perrot was never granted a permanent position. Turning more and more to choreography, Perrot then went to London where he created "Alma", "Lalla Rookh" and many other ballets, probably the most famous of which was "Pas de Quatre", noteworthy as the first ballet which featured four of the leading ballerinas of the day in the same work. It was successful as a work of art as well as a work of diplomacy which insured harmony among four rival stars.

Perhaps his greatest effort was also one for which he got no credit, that of choreographing the "Giselle" solos for Grisi. She rose to stardom in the role Perrot created and it is here that he infused the combination of dancing, mime and acting that has made the role quite possibly the first great dramatic part for a ballerina.

From 1814 through 1858 Perrot was dancer, choreographer and ballet master at St. Petersburg's Imperial Theatre. There he restaged his previous works and created eight new ballets before being forced to leave the country because of his political convictions. Europe had changed greatly since his departure for Russia; he never again found the fame he had once enjoyed and died, practically forgotten, in 1892.

Arthur Saint-Léon

(1821-1870)

"The Father of Folk Ballet"

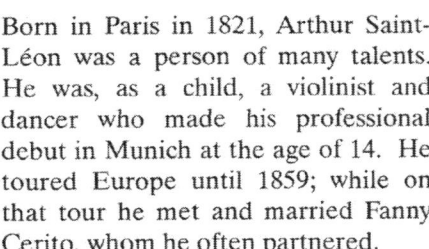

Born in Paris in 1821, Arthur Saint-Léon was a person of many talents. He was, as a child, a violinist and dancer who made his professional debut in Munich at the age of 14. He toured Europe until 1859; while on that tour he met and married Fanny Cerito, whom he often partnered.

Saint-Léon's many talents enhanced his work at the Paris Opéra Ballet, first as choreographer (1847-1852) and then as ballet master (1863-1870). He composed music, devised a system of dance notation, even created sets and costumes. He developed a flair for the presentation of lightly comic ballets, particularly those with character or folk dances incorporated into them. His first work as a choreographer was "La Fille de Marbre", which he created for Fanny Cerito's Paris debut in 1847.

In 1859 Saint-Léon became ballet master of the Imperial Theatre in St. Petersburg, succeeding Jules Perrot, and was there until 1867. While in Russia, Saint-Léon created "Mariquita" (1860), "The Nymphs and the Stayr" (1861) and "The Humpbacked Horse" (1866). It was with this last ballet that Saint-Léon made what would be his great contribution to ballet. "The Humpbacked Horse" was a Russian folk tale; Saint-Léon created a ballet around it in order to give Russian audiences, weary of the same ballets, something new and different. Into it he choreographed folk dances from many parts of Russia.

This success paved the way for Saint-Léon's lasting treasure. "Coppélia", his last ballet, is based on a tale by E.T.A. Hoffmann. Choreographed in 1870 for the Paris Opéra, it is a comic masterpiece with Saint-Léon's trademark folk dances incorporated into the story. Featuring Hungarian czardas, Polish mazurkas and dances capturing the Scottish and Spanish heritages, "Coppélia" marked the end of the Romantic period and the demise of France's supremacy in the world of ballet.

The Franco-Prussian War broke out just shortly after the premiere of "Coppélia"; Saint-Léon died during the siege of Paris at the age of 49.

Luckily, "Coppélia" lives on, a happy tribute to Saint-Léon's talent and a perfect showcase for his trademark - colorful, local realism highlighted by lively folk dances.

Fanny Cerito

(1817-1909)
"The Neopolitan"

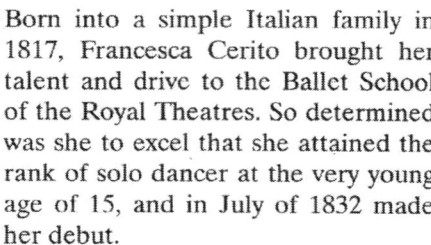

Born into a simple Italian family in 1817, Francesca Cerito brought her talent and drive to the Ballet School of the Royal Theatres. So determined was she to excel that she attained the rank of solo dancer at the very young age of 15, and in July of 1832 made her debut.

Cerito's performances were quite successful and led to tours in Rome, Florence and Naples. Her first major engagement outside Italy was in Vienna, Austria. While there she was given the affectionate nickname of Fanny; she used this version of her name for the rest of her life.

Cerito became prima ballerina at La Scala in 1838 and performed there for two years. During that period she studied under Carlo Blasis, one of the most talented teachers of the 19th century and a pioneer of the "Italian technique", which survives today. 1840 found Cerito in London for her debut there. Her technique was spectacular, her stage presence was charming and London was captivated by the young Italian ballerina.

While in London Cerito was partnered by Arthur Saint-Léon. Their stage partnership soon became a personal partnership and the two were married in Paris in 1845.

In July of that year Cerito made what would become one of her most famous appearances. She, with three of the other most noted ballerinas of the period, Marie Taglioni, Lucile Grahn and Carlotta Grisi, danced the trend-setting "Pas de Quatre". The ballet was unique in that it was the first time four leading ballerinas appeared on stage together.

Cerito and Saint-Léon made their last tour together in 1851. After the Madrid engagement, Cerito returned to London while Saint-Léon continued his career in Paris and Russia.

In 1855, Cerito finally made an appearance in Russia. Past her prime as a dancer, she was upstaged by a young Russian ballerina, Bogdanova, who had been Saint-Léon's pupil in Paris. Disillusioned by that and by the Russians' nationalistic non-acceptance of things foreign, Cerito left for England in 1857 to retire.

Cerito lived in comfort for over fifty more years, remaining involved with the ballet world. She died at the age of 91 in 1909. Although never a meteoric star, Cerito remains memorable as one of the Romantic period's great talents.

Lucile Grahn
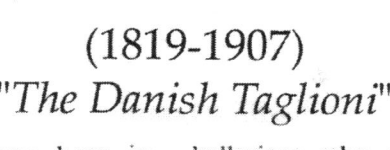

(1819-1907)
"The Danish Taglioni"

Lucina Alexia Grahn was born in Copenhagen, Denmark, in 1819 and studied at the Royal Danish Ballet School. In 1829, when Grahn was 10, Auguste Bournonville returned to Denmark as the director of the Royal Ballet School and quickly took notice of the talented child. He took a personal interest in Grahn's progress and, when she was 15, arranged for her to study in Paris.

It was in 1836 that she became a star. Bournonville produced "La Sylphide" in Copenhagen and Grahn created the title role. Although a true Scandinavian, tall, slim and blond, she brought her own touch to the role and became known in her country as "the Danish Taglioni".

Grahn left Denmark in 1839 to dance at the Paris Opéra but her career there was cut short because of a knee injury. In 1843 she went to Russia, one of the few ballerinas to appear there while still quite young. Appearing immediately after Taglioni, who was older, she was a more appealing Sylphide and was well received by the Russian public.

In 1844 Grahn made 40 appearances in Milan and then went to England where her career blossomed during the five years she stayed there. She was the youngest of the four ballerinas who performed "Pas de Quatre" in 1845 and, as such, danced the first variation in the landmark ballet. Perrot created several ballets for her, including "Catarina" and "Lalla Rookh", and through these ballets Grahn's acting skills reached new heights. Perrot believed that her talent extended beyond the romantic roles to include character parts.

Returning to Germany, where her first successes abroad had been staged, Grahn first performed, then elected to retire there. Settling in Munich, she married Friederich Young in 1856. Her husband, a tenor, suffered a spinal injury from a fall in 1863 and was paralyzed. Grahn, forced to make a living to take care of her invalid husband, began teaching privately. She then was appointed teacher at the Munich Hoftheater. She expanded her career by choreographing a number of divertissements for operas, one of the most successful being "Bacchanale" for Richard Wagner's "Tannhauser".

Grahn outlived her husband by 23 years and died in 1907. Her legacy to ballet was not only what she accomplished during her career, but also what was accomplished after her death. Having no heirs, Grahn left her estate to the city of Munich to be used for helping young, talented artists.

Mathilde Kschessinska

(1872-1971)
"The Princess"

Born into a noble Polish family just outside St. Petersburg, Russia, in 1872, Kschessinska was the daughter of Felix Kschessinski, who was a character dancer at the Maryinsky Theatre. Continuing a multi-generation family tradition of being in the theatre, Kschessinska entered the Imperial Ballet School in 1880 at the age of 8. She studied first under Lev Ivanov, then under Catherine Vazem and, at the age of 15, entered the class of Christian Johansen where she found the inspiration that sparked her career.

In 1890 she made her debut at the Maryinsky, dancing the pas de deux from "La Fille Mal Gardée", and in 1895 was granted the status of prima ballerina assoluta. She was a favorite of the Imperial family and, through the many years of her reign, gained much wealth, power and influence. She danced "La Sylphide", "Sleeping Beauty", "Swan Lake" and many other ballets in the classical repertoire and is credited with being the first Russian ballerina to ever execute the 32 fouettés first introduced by Legnani.

A brief and star-crossed romance with the Tsarevitch, who would become the ill-fated Nicholas I, last Tsar of Russia, ended unhappily with his engagement to Princess Alice of Hesse-Coburg (Alexandra). At the age of 28 she met and fell in love with Grand Duke Andre Vladimirovitch; they married many years later in 1921. The marriage earned for her the title of Princess Romanovsky-Krassinsky.

Hers was a life of great wealth, influence and privilege until the years of the Russian Revolution and World War I. In 1917 she and Grand Duke Andre, like many of the Russian aristocracy, fled the country and settled in Paris. News of the massacre of the Russian Royal Family ended any hopes of returning to their native land.

Kschessinska, to make a living for her family, opened a ballet school in Paris and began her career as a teacher. As she had been particularly noted for her presentation as much as her technique, she set about imparting that showmanship to her students, including the young Margot Fonteyn, and was quite successful.

Her last appearance was in 1935 with the Ballet Russe de Monte Carlo in London. Her memoirs of a most unusual and exciting life were published in 1960. She died in Paris in 1971, leaving the ballet world not only the legacy of her training, but also with a vivid memory of this last great prima ballerina assoluta who reigned triumphant in a glittering world now found only in the pages of history.

The Ballet Book

History

The History of Ballet

I. Origins

The history of dancing is as old as the history of humans. Ballet with its movements from the graceful arabesque to the electrifying grand jeté had its beginnings, as did all other dance forms, in the rhythmic movements of primitive ritual. Refined movement, becoming a more skilled discipline, was an integral part of the religious rites of ancient cultures around the world.

Western civilization credits the ancient Greek culture with bringing the first story dances as part of masked Greek drama, and the use of masks remained in theatrical dances until the late 18th century. The Romans expanded on these story dances, incorporating fables and adding the comic aspects of acrobatics to dance and mime. This much more lighthearted approach to dance soon eclipsed the idea of dance or rhythmic movement as an element solely of religious ritual or Greek tragedy.

II. The Renaissance

The comic art of the Romans resurfaced in 16th century Italy with the "commedia dell'arte", comic routines built around stock characters (Columbine, Harlequin, Pierrot, Pulcinella, Punch) and performed by the first "traveling companies". While this was flourishing around the Italian and French countryside, the capital cities of Europe were staging elaborate pageants and entertainments in their royal courts, including masked dancing by court members.

The court entertainments and pageantry of Italy frequently centered around mythology and successfully combined pantomime, dancing and song into what was usually called "ballet"; however, it would take another two centuries for ballet as we know it to become a separate discipline. Ballet is defined as that discipline of the dance noted by the turning out of the dancers' feet and virtually all steps arising from one of five basic positions. The word "ballet" evolved from the Italian "ballare" (to dance).

Catherine de Medici, the Italian queen of France, is credited with bringing this story dancing and

pageantry to the French court on October 15, 1581. She and an Italian violinist staged an elaborate entertainment depicting the life of Circe - it lasted for five and a half hours and is considered to be the first ballet, a production melding the elements of dance, music, plot and design.

Just seven years later (1588) a book was published in France by Thoinot Arbeau that outlined the principles for the five basic positions of the feet and the basic steps to prepare the body for specific movement - the foundation upon which classical ballet was based.

Court ballet continued to flourish in France. King Louis XIV was an accomplished dancer himself and enjoyed performing in the ballets. As King, he nearly always portrayed a god or royal personage, and his frequent appearances as Apollo, the sun god, were partially responsible for his being referred to as the "Sun King". His major contribution to ballet, though, was the establishment in 1669 of an academy of dance which still exists today as the Paris Opéra Ballet. Pierre Beauchamps, the first ballet master at the Paris Opéra,

formally established and named Arbeau's five basic positions and, thus, moved dance from a court pastime into a profession.

Until late in the 16th century, young boys had danced the female roles as it was not considered proper for ladies to appear on the theatre stage. But in 1681 a new era in ballet was introduced by the Academie director with a dance featuring four female dancers. Mlle. Lafontaine was one of these dancers and is considered to be the first professional ballerina.

It was during this time that Pierre Rameau codified the five positions of the feet (1725) and ballet "left the ground" as aerial techniques were developed, establishing ballet forever as its own art form.

III. The 18th Century

This was the era of the great male dancer. Unencumbered by the weighty wigs and long skirts that were required female costuming, the male dancer developed excellence in the techniques of turns and jumps. Gaetan Vestris (1729-1808) was considered the greatest male dancer of his time. His influence on male dancing extended on into the next century by way of his son, Auguste Vestris (1760-1842). Trained by his father, Auguste was the premier danseur and renowned teacher at the Paris Opéra for almost 36 years. At 75 years of age, Auguste made his last appearance partnering Marie Taglioni.

Auguste Vestris had, in turn, continued the training of Auguste Bournonville (1805-1879), who had begun his studies under his own father at the Royal Danish Ballet School. Bournonville returned to Denmark taking with him the tradition of male dance excellence. A gifted dancer and choreographer, he contributed the legacy of brilliantly executed male roles, thus establishing a distinctive national character which continues to be the hallmark of today's Royal Danish Ballet.

Marie Camargo (La Camargo) scandalously shortened the dancer's skirt to calf length in the early 1700s, allowing more mobility. She also removed the heels from her dancing slippers in order to show off her jumps and light step. A little later Marie Sallé loosened her skirt and bodice, giving an entirely new freedom of expression for the female dancers.

During this period (1760) literature was published by Jean Georges Noverre calling for a greater naturalism in ballet and a more logical relationship between the dance step and corresponding point in the story. He also wished to see the masks, wigs and panniers (an early hoopskirt) banished from the ballet. His theories led the way to the ballet d'action, where the element of dance became secondary to the expression of the story in pantomime.

IV. The 19th Century - The Romantic Ballet

The Romantic movement in 19th century literature produced the plots for the romantic ballet. Stories of unearthly and enchanted creatures abounded and the ballets of the era brought forth two features that remain an integral part of ballet today.

A little-known ballet produced in 1823, "The Fairy and the Knight", seems to have provided the first appearance of dancing on pointe, the technical innovation that has become the primary feature of female classical ballet dancing. Introduced by Amalia

Brugnoli in the leading role, pointe dancing seems to have been inspired by the ballet of the period and was quickly adopted by the Italian, French and Russian schools.

Dancing on pointe was assured of its permanence in ballet when Marie Taglioni, the epitome of the ethereal ballerina, brought it to her performance in "La Sylphide" in 1832. Because her soft ballet slippers were stitched around the toes on the outside with, perhaps, some soft cotton inside, Taglioni's pointe work was confined to a few graceful poses. It is believed that Carlotta Grisi was first to use a boxed slipper similar to today's blocked pointe shoes.

"La Sylphide" was considered Taglioni's greatest role and the ballet influenced the fashion styles of the day with sylphide coiffures, dresses, flowers and moods. It also influenced the fashion of ballet. In it, and also introduced by La Taglioni, first appeared the long, white tutu. Because of the romantic subject matter of the ballets, this costume became traditional for the dancers of the period. In fact, many of the ballets referred to today as the "white ballets" ("Les Sylphides", "Giselle", "Swan Lake") are so called due to the influence of these filmy white costumes from the Romantic period.

Augusta Maywood is considered the first ballerina from the United States. She came from Philadelphia and made her debut at the Paris Opéra in 1839.

Fanny Elssler, one of the five most notable dancers of the era, was Austrian by birth but became known for the passionate, fiery regional dances of Spain and Italy. She never possessed the elevation for which La Taglioni set the standard and, therefore, disappointed the audiences of the Paris Opéra when she danced "La Sylphide". But her tours of the United States, Europe and Russia were great successes and she had a strong, faithful following.

The other four famous Romantic Age ballerinas (Marie Taglioni, Carlotta Grisi, Lucile Grahn and Fanny Cerito) danced together in "Pas de Quatre" performed in London in 1845. The dance was choreographed by Jules Perrot especially for these dancers, and temperaments flared over the question of who would dance the next to last variation, since it was without question that La Taglioni would have the honored last position. Benjamin Lumley, manager of Her Majesty's Theatre and a master diplomat, suggested that the matter be settled according to age....and suddenly each was courteously offering to lead. Grahn, the youngest, led; followed by Grisi, less than a year older; Cerrito, two years older and La Taglioni who, being the eldest, maintained the place of honor.

The Romantic Age produced two other famous ballets still performed today, "Giselle" (1841) and "Coppélia" (1870).

"Giselle" was choreographed by Jean Coralli, but Jules Perrot was responsible for the choreography of the role of Giselle, danced by Carlotta Grisi. Although the original choreography has been lost, the version most often seen today is based on the one produced in 1860 by Marius Petipa.

Arthur Saint-Léon was only 49 years old when he choreographed his greatest ballet "Coppélia", dying only three months after its premiere. The ballet is noted for its character dances such as Polish mazurkas, Hungarian czardas and Scottish, Spanish and Chinese doll dances.

V. The 19th Century - The Italian Ballet

The Italian ballet is primarily noted for technique. Italian dancers frequently brought exceptional techniques that were choreographed into other country's ballets to showcase them. Pierina Legnani was the first ballerina to accomplish 32 consecutive fouettés. When she premiered the Ivanov/Petipa version of the ballet "Swan Lake", she injected her impressive feat into the choreography of the Black Swan Pas de Deux.

It remains a tour de force for today's ballerina.

The Italian ballet was also responsible for noted teachers of technique. In 1830 Carlo Blasis, a former dancer himself and director of La Scala's Royal Academy of the Dance, published *The Code of Terpsichore*, which outlined a system of ballet technique. Enrico Cecchetti, the coach of Nijinsky and Pavlova, studied with a student of Blasis. He brought, with minor variations, the Italian technique into the twentieth century.

VI. *The 19th Century - The Russian Classical Ballet*

By the late 1800s the French ballet was on the decline and Russia became the ballet center of the world. The Russian Imperial School had been founded in 1735 by Empress Anna Ivanovna who brought the French Jean-Baptiste Lande and the Italian Francesco Araya to instruct cadet sons of noblemen. In 1801, another Frenchman, Charles-Louis Didelot, became choreographer at the Imperial Theatre and he set out a firm syllabus for teaching. He is known as the father of Russian ballet. Didelot was followed by Jules Perrot (from 1848 to 1858), Arthur Saint-Léon (1859 to 1870) and Marius Petipa (1870 to 1903).

Marius Petipa arrived in St. Petersburg from France in 1847. First engaged as a dancer, he became ballet master of the Imperial Theatre in 1870, for a career that spanned more than 50 years. As ballet master he virtually single-handedly created the classical Russian repertoire. He created over 50 new ballets, revised 17 others and mounted ballets in 34 operas.

Probably the most famous works created by Petipa and his gifted assistant, Lev Ivanov, are "Swan Lake", "The Sleeping Beauty" and "The Nutcracker", each in collaboration with the composer Peter Ilyich Tchaikovsky.

Enrico Cecchetti (1850-1928) was engaged as premier danseur and teacher at the Imperial Maryinsky Theatre in St. Petersburg in 1887. As a dancer he created the dual roles of the Blue Bird and the wicked Carabosse in "The Sleeping Beauty", the Charlatan in "Petrouchka" and Pantalon in "Le Carnaval". As a teacher he gave to the Russian ballet the brilliant techniques of the Italian Academy of Dance.

The last Imperial prima ballerina assoluta was Mathilde Kschessinska who reigned for 27 years on the stage of the Maryinsky. She is credited with being the first Russian dancer to master the Italian technique of executing 32 fouettés.

VII. *Changing Times*

World events were about to change the opulent world of ballet as then known. Russia was on the verge of a revolution against the Tsar and his government that would see the Imperial Ballet in St. Petersburg crashing into a decline. The revolution would also send many Russian dancers to the West with the help of Diaghilev's Ballets Russes. World Wars I and II would set up barriers that would make Russian ballet all but disappear from view to the rest of the world. However, in the West, the history of ballet continued. Just as the center of ballet moved from France to Russia, it would soon find its way to America, and, in so doing, would eventually make America the new ballet capital of the world.

The Ballet Book

The Ballets

La Fille Mal Gardée

Music: Johann Wilhelm Hertel
Choreography and Libretto: Jean (Bercher) Dauberval
First presented: 1786, Bordeaux, France

Ballet in three scenes. This is considered to be the oldest ballet still in production. However, very little, if any, of Dauberval's original choreography has survived. Jean Bercher, who had studied with Noverre, used the professional name of Dauberval and has been referred to as the father of comic ballet. Fanny Elssler used it as her farewell performance in New York on November 12, 1842. Many revisions of this ballet have been made by such experts as Auguste Bournonville, Mikhail Mordkin and Bronislava Nijinska.

SCENE I. In a rural French village, a widow, Madame Simone, gossips with her neighbors. As they leave, taking her with them, Madam Simone's daughter, Lisette, comes out of the cottage to water her plants. Colin, her sweetheart, enters carrying his rake. Lisette and Colin dance but are interrupted by Madame Simone, who does not approve of Colin. She chases him off and begins to scold her daughter for her flirtation. Some of Lisette's friends enter and ask her to join them in their dance. With Madame Simone's permission, Lisette begins to dance with them. Colin has sneaked in and hidden behind some people, but as soon as Madame Simone leaves, he pushes forward and surprises Lisette. They dance again, and again Madame Simone returns to find them together and chases Colin off. Lisette, in a temper, stomps her feet and shakes her fists and cries as her mother tries to calm her. Colin appears behind Madame Simone and Lisette waves to him. Madame Simone sends Colin off and sits her daughter down to work at a butter churn. Lisette begins to churn and her mother leaves her to her work. Colin slips up behind Lisette and starts to churn the butter with her. Lisette then dances for Colin, and at the end Colin throws her a lovely long ribbon. The two dance, entwining themselves with the ribbon. They then leave the stage.

Thomas, a wealthy vinegrower, has come to see Madame Simone regarding the marriage contract between her daughter and his butterfly-catching son, Alain. Agreements are made and the parents are delighted. Lisette and Alain are pushed together. The curtain closes as Lisette and Alain realize the situation their parents have just arranged and they are both horrified.

SCENE II. Out on the village green, the harvest festival is taking place. The villagers and some gypsies dance. Alain and Lisette are made to stand together to watch. Madame Simone, having decided that Thomas might be a good match for her, flirts with him. Thomas asks her to dance and off they go. Lisette quickly goes over to Colin and explains to him the situation was not her idea, but her mother's. They dance a sweet adagio followed by their two variations.

Alain enters chasing butterflies with his net and two village girls try to dance with him. Just then thunder is heard, lightning flashes are seen and everyone runs for cover from the rain as the curtain closes.

SCENE III. To escape the storm, Lisette and her mother quickly enter their cottage. Madame Simone settles down

La Fille Mal Gardée

at her spinning wheel, but she soon becomes very sleepy. Lisette, having seen Colin at the window, tries to leave, but her mother wakes up. Lisette asks her mother to play the tambourine so she can dance; however, Madame Simone is not aware that Lisette is dancing for Colin.

A group of villagers enter with sheaves of wheat and stack them against a table. Lisette tries to leave with them but her mother catches her. Madame Simone tells her to do some work at the spinning-wheel and leaves, locking Lisette in the room. Dreaming of Colin, Lisette dances and imagines herself married to him. Suddenly, the sheaves of wheat are thrown aside and there stands Colin. Embarrassed, Lisette quarrels with Colin, but they make up and exchange scarves as tokens of their love.

Lisette hears Madame Simone coming and pushes Colin into the hayloft. Her mother quickly notices the scarf and is furious at her daughter. Just then Thomas and Alain arrive with the notary and some friends to sign the marriage contract. As a precaution, Madame Simone locks Lisette in the hayloft.

As the business is discussed, Madame Simone gives Alain the key and tells him where to find his bride. Alain unlocks the door and finds Lisette and Colin, their clothes and hair covered with hay. Madame Simone is scandalized that the family reputation has been ruined. But as the lovers kneel before her and explain, Madame Simone realizes that the notary is already there and so finally consents to the marriage between Lisette and Colin.

La Sylphide

Music: Jean Schneitzhoeffer
Choreography: Philippe Taglioni
Scenery: Pierre Ciceri
Costumes: Eugene Lami
Book: Adolphe Nourrit
First presented: March 12, 1832, Paris Opéra with Marie Taglioni as La Sylphide and Joseph Mazilier as James

Ballet in two acts. This is the ballet that ushered in the era of the Romantic ballet. Choreographed by her father, it made Marie Taglioni famous, Marie Taglioni made the ballet famous, and the ethereal, long, white tutu was made famous. It was also in this ballet that Marie Taglioni is credited with popularizing the use of pointe work. Marie Taglioni and "La Sylphide" remained inseparable in those years, and Marie had the title and honor of being known as "La Taglioni". In 1836 Auguste Bournonville created another version of "La Sylphide" for the Royal Danish Ballet. Lucile Grahn originally danced the role, for which she became known as the "Danish Taglioni". The ballet is still performed as part of the Royal Danish repertoire; however, today's accepted version of the ballet is an approximation of Bournonville's as his original choreography (as well as Taglioni's) has been lost.

ACT I. The curtain opens on the interior of an 1830s Scottish farmhouse on the wedding day of James and Effie. Asleep in the winged chair by the large fireplace is James Reuben and in the corner by the fireplace is Gurn, another young peasant, who is also asleep.

Dressed in his wedding kilt, James seems restless in his sleep. His dream, a beautiful Sylphide, is kneeling at his feet. She flutters around and lightly kisses him on the forehead. James awakens suddenly and, startled at the sight, reaches out for her. But she dashes towards the fireplace and vanishes.

Not understanding if he really saw her, James shakes Gurn awake and asks him. Gurn, who is in love with Effie, had been dreaming about her but does not want to admit that to James. They are interrupted by the arrival of Effie and James' mother. Gurn greets Effie, but she wonders why James is so distant. Shaking off his thoughts, James greets her with a kiss.

Neighbors and bridesmaids arrive with gifts. Gurn begs some of Effie's friends to speak for him, but they put him off and go on presenting Effie with her wedding gifts.

Unnoticed by the group, James has been drawn over to the fireplace where the Sylphide vanished. Suddenly from the shadows comes the old hag, Madge, the village sorceress. James orders her away, but the girls run to her and ask her to tell their fortunes. Effie holds out the palm of her hand and Madge tells her that she will be married, but not to James. In a rage, James drives her from the house.

Mother Reuben tells Effie and her bridesmaids that it is time to prepare for the wedding and leads them upstairs. The other guests leave and James is alone in the room. He turns and sees the Sylphide in the window. She seems to float down. As they dance she tells James that she loves him, but he reminds her that he will marry Effie this day. The Sylphide, despondent, bids him farewell. Overcome by her tears, James confesses that he loves her. The Sylphide, dancing for joy, calls James to follow her. He is reluctant to

La Sylphide

move. The Sylphide picks up the plaid left behind by Effie, puts it around her shoulders and poses as the bride. At that, James can no longer resist and when the Sylphide kneels at his feet, he picks her up and kisses her.

Gurn, hidden by shadows, has seen the whole episode and rushes up the stairs to Effie. Hearing the noise, James hides the Sylphide in the chair, covering her with the plaid. Everyone enters and Gurn accuses James of faithlessness with another woman in the room. Gurns pulls the plaid off the chair but there is nothing there. The Sylphide has again vanished. Effie scolds Gurn for his jealousy.

Wedding guests arrive to begin the festivities. Dancing begins and when James and Effie dance, the others stand away to watch. Suddenly the Sylphide, whom only James can see, changes their pas de deux into a pas de trois. And when the guests join in the dancing, James tries not to lose sight of the Sylphide as she darts in and out among the people.

The guests prepare for the wedding ceremony. As James and Effie begin to exchange wedding rings, the ring James holds in his hand suddenly disappears. The Sylphide has snatched it from his hand and, declaring that she will die if he marries another, vanishes. James rushes to follow her.

Effie is heartbroken and in tears. As Gurn enters he says that he saw James running off with another woman. The curtain closes as Effie sits in the winged chair by the fireplace with the plaid around her shoulders and Gurn kneeling at her feet.

ACT II. The scene opens on a dark, misty forest glen where a fire casts ominous reflections of the old hag, Madge, and her evil sister witches by their cave. They dance around the cauldron as Madge makes incantational signs over the potion brewing inside. Silencing them, Madge pokes her crooked stick into the cauldron and lifts out a beautiful gossamer scarf. Madge and the witches retreat into their cave.

Dawn has arrived and James enters carrying a bird's nest. He looks about and suddenly the Sylphide appears. He offers her his gift, but she is appalled that it is a living gift and immediately replaces it in a tree branch. Before James can take her fully in his arms, the Sylphide calls for her sisters to join them and they all dance. But, whenever James reaches for his love, she is quickly replaced by one of the others. He can never seem to hold her. One by one they vanish until James is alone.

A noise startles him and he is surprised to see Madge. Remembering his rudeness to her the day before, he apologizes. She asks why he looks so sad and he explains that whenever he reaches out to his love, she eludes him. Madge offers her help and presents James with the magic scarf. She tells him to gently place the scarf around the Sylphide's shoulders and she will never again fly away from him.

James is delighted. Madge, knowing her awful secret, gleefully hurries back into her cave as the Sylphide approaches. James and the Sylphide dance and he presents her with his new gift. As he gently encircles her with the scarf, the Sylphide shudders in pain. Her wings fall off and she clutches at her heart. James, astonished at what is happening, rushes to hold her in his arms. But the Sylphide pushes him away in horror and dies.

Kneeling beside her, James weeps as the other sylphs carry off the body of their sister. Madge's hideous cackle is heard as revenge is hers.

James, alone with his grief, is aware of the stirring bagpipes and joyous bells ringing as the bridal procession of Effie and Gurn makes its way along a path in the distance as the curtain closes.

Giselle

Music: Adolphe Adam
Choreography: Jean Coralli and Jules Perrot
Book: Vernoy de Saint-Georges, Théophile Gautier and Jean Coralli
Scenery: Pierre Ciceri
Costumes: Paul Lormier
First Presented: June 28, 1841, Paris Opéra with Carlotta Grisi as Giselle, Lucien Petipa as Albrecht, Adèle Dumilâtre as Myrtha, Queen of the Wilis

Ballet in two acts. Giselle is to the dancer what Hamlet is to the actor. It is one of the oldest, continually performed ballets in history. The legend of the Wilis, from a book by Heinrich Heine, was used as the basis from which a complete libretto was written and accepted within three days by the Paris Opéra, and within a week Adam had written the music.

ACT I. It is vintage time in the Rhine and everyone in the village is busy preparing for the harvest festival. Hilarion, a gamekeeper, enters and stops at Giselle's cottage. Before he can knock he hears a noise. He runs across the stage and hides beside a hut. Albrecht, a duke in disguise, and his squire, Wilfred, enter. Albrecht, known to the villagers as Loys, removes his royal cloak and sword and tells Wilfred to hide them in the hut. Albrecht, like Hilarion, is in love with Giselle. After Wilfred puts the cloak and sword in the hut, he tries once more to persuade Albrecht to leave. But Albrecht refuses and dismisses Wilfred.

Albrecht knocks on Giselle's door, and then playfully hides around the corner of her cottage as she comes out. He surprises her and they continue to play and dance. Giselle picks a flower and begins the loves-me-loves-me-not test, but it ends on loves-me-not and she throws it down. Albrecht picks it up and pulls each petal out declaring loves-me for each one. They continue to dance.

Hilarion interrupts and declares his love for Giselle. She is startled by this and tells him that she does not return his affection, but he continues to plead with her. Albrecht

warns Hilarion to leave Giselle alone, and as Hilarion turns to leave, he threatens Albrecht.

The villagers enter and soon engage Giselle and Albrecht in their lively dances. Giselle's mother, Berthe, comes out of the cottage and warns her to stop dancing because of her frail heart. She tells them about the legend that says if a young girl dies before her wedding day, she will become one of the Wilis, a restless band of ghosts doomed to dance every night hounding to death all who cross their paths. Giselle obeys her mother and goes into the cottage to rest.

Hilarion returns to try once again to talk to Giselle, but as he approaches her cottage, a horn sounds to announce the arrival of the hunting party of the Prince of Courland, and his daughter, Bathilde. As they pass Giselle's cottage, the Prince tells Wilfred, who is with the hunting party, that they are in need of some refreshments and to knock on the cottage door. Berthe and Giselle welcome the royal party and bring out refreshments. Fascinated by the rich clothes the Princess is wearing, Giselle gently touches the hem of Bathilde's gown to her cheek. Bathilde, amused by this, gives Giselle her necklace. The royal party accepts Berthe's

Giselle

invitation to rest and they retire into the cottage.

The villagers, having chosen Giselle as Queen of the Vintage, ask her to join in their dancing. Suddenly Hilarion runs out and, with vengeance, tells Giselle that Albrecht is not Loys, the peasant, but Albrecht, Duke of Silesia. Showing Giselle the royal cloak and sword, Hilarion blows the hunting horn to call the hunting party out. The Prince and Bathilde come out of the cottage and are surprised to find Albrecht there dressed in peasant clothes. Albrecht kneels to Bathilde and kisses her hand. Giselle, rushing forward, pushes Bathilde away telling her that she is engaged to him. Bathilde tells Giselle that she, too, is engaged to Albrecht.

Stunned, Giselle begins to realize the truth. Her mind wanders back to happier times as she retraces the moments spent with her love. She stumbles across Albrecht's sword, which had fallen to the ground when Wilfred saved Albrecht from harming Hilarion with it. Giselle picks it up and drags it around in a circle. Everyone is frozen in disbelief. Giselle lifts the sword high, but before Albrecht can reach her, she stabs herself. Hilarion, realizing the harm his jealousy has done, kneels and weeps. As Giselle is dying, Albrecht swears his eternal love for her.

ACT II. The scene is late at night in a misty glade where Giselle is buried. Myrtha, Queen of the Wilis, with her band of Wilis, come to initiate Giselle. The veiled figure of Myrtha glides across the stage. Through eerie, yet beautiful dancing, Myrtha brings forth the other Wilis and then calls Giselle from her grave. Slowly Giselle moves toward the Queen and bows to her. Myrtha touches Giselle with her magic branches, commands her to begin dancing and disburses the Wilis to search the forest for intruders.

Albrecht enters to mourn at Giselle's grave and, as he kneels there, he feels the cold touch of a hand and senses Giselle's ghost. Turning, he sees her and tries to catch her but she floats away. He follows her deeper into the forest.

Hilarion now enters and comes to Giselle's grave to seek her forgiveness, but the Wilis find and encircle him. Pleading for mercy from Myrtha and the Wilis, he is ruthlessly thrown into the lake and drowned.

The Wilis have also discovered Albrecht in the forest and Giselle tells him to take refuge on her grave for there Myrtha is powerless to harm him. But, Myrtha, in full command of Giselle, tells her she must entice him off her grave to dance with her. Giselle must obey. No amount of pleading by Giselle and Albrecht will melt Myrtha's icy will. Their pas de deux is ethereal and hauntingly lovely. Myrtha again orders them to dance. Albrecht falls from exhaustion only to be revived to continue dancing. Giselle pleads for his life again and again. Myrtha's answer is always the same. Albrecht dances on and on, then collapses a final time.

A distant bell chimes the time of dawn and heralds that the Wilis must return to their graves, for they are powerless during the day. Albrecht's life has been spared. The Wilis and Myrtha glide away. Now Albrecht and Giselle must say good-bye forever. He cradles her in his arms one last time, then she fades back into her grave. Albrecht is left alone and in despair falls to the ground as the curtain closes.

The Nutcracker

Music: Peter Ilyich Tchaikovsky
Choreography: Lev Ivanov
Book: Lev Ivanov after E.T.A. Hoffmann's "The Nutcracker and The Mouse King"
Scenery: M.I. Botcharov
First presented: December 17, 1892, Russian Imperial Ballet, Maryinsky Theatre, St. Petersburg, with Antonietta dell-Era as the Sugar Plum Fairy and Paul Gerdt as her Cavalier

Ballet in two acts. This Christmas ballet is Tchaikovsky's third and last ballet score. Unique to this score is that in the snow scene there is a singing chorus, although not all versions of the music use this part of the score. Tchaikovsky also employed the new instrument, the celesta, into the music for the dance of the Sugar Plum Fairy.

ACT I, SCENE I. The ballet begins at a Christmas party in the home of Clara, her brother, Fritz, and their parents. The guests are the family's friends, young and old. The children dance for their elders and the grown-ups also dance during the evening. Clara's godfather, Herr Drosselmeyer, has given her a most wonderful gift, a nutcracker modeled as a handsome soldier. She loves it, but Fritz teases her and in roughhousing with her over it, the nutcracker gets broken. Clara is heartbroken. Herr Drosselmeyer wraps his kerchief around the nutcracker's jaw and Clara consoles the doll as she puts it down under the Christmas tree. It is time for Clara, Fritz, and the rest of the children to go to bed. The party ends and the guests leave. The family retires upstairs to bed. But Clara is so worried about her nutcracker that after all the lights are out and the house is quiet she slips downstairs to check on him.

As Clara moves quietly into the room, she hears a noise. A battle is raging between an army of toy soldiers, led by her Nutcracker, against an army of mice, led by their seven-headed king. The soldiers fight bravely, but the mice seem to be winning. Clara, seeing that the Nutcracker is in trouble, throws her shoe at the Mouse King and helps the Nutcracker win the battle.

In a gesture of gratitude for her help, the Nutcracker bows to Clara; however, he is no longer a toy nutcracker soldier, he is a handsome prince. To reward Clara, he offers to take her on a journey to the beautiful Kingdom of Sweets. The stage darkens as he leads her on their way.

ACT I, SCENE II. The scene opens with soft, snowy light as Clara and the Prince travel by sleigh through the falling snow. On the way, the Snow King and Snow Queen come forth to greet the young travelers. The snowflakes waltz and flurry all around them. After the King and Queen dance their pas de deux for Clara and the Prince, they send them on to continue their journey.

ACT II. This act takes place inside the palace of the Kingdom of Sweets. Clara and the Prince are met by the beautiful Sugar Plum Fairy. The Prince tells her how Clara helped him in the battle with the Mouse King. To celebrate and pay tribute to Clara, the Sugar Plum Fairy leads her to sit upon a throne, with her Prince by her side. A series of divertissements in the form of court entertainment begins first with Hot Chocolate, a lively Spanish dance, followed by Coffee, an Arabian dance. Then there's Tea, the energetic Chinese dance, and the strong Russian Trepak. Candy Canes and Marzipan Shepherdesses dance. Mother Ginger

arrives wearing a huge hoop-skirt and opens the front panels of her skirts so the little Polichinelles can come out to perform their peppy dances. Next comes the colorful Waltz of the Flowers. But the moment everyone has waited for now arrives as the Sugar Plum Fairy and her Cavalier perform their beautiful pas de deux. As the ballet ends, the entire court joins the Sugar Plum Fairy and her Cavalier to dance a final tribute to Clara. As they all bow to her, Clara is sure this is the most wonderful Christmas she has ever had.

Pas De Quatre

Music: Cesare Pugni
Choreography: Jules Perrot
First presented: July 12, 1845, His Majesty's Theatre, London
with Marie Taglioni, Fanny Cerito, Carlotta Grisi, Lucile Grahn

This historic short ballet is famous for presenting four of the greatest ballerinas of its time dancing on stage together. Perrot was given, possibly, the most formidable task ever expected of a ballet master. He was charged with inventing an ensemble piece for these rival ballerinas and devising solos for each one that would display their individual artistry, without any one upstaging the others. The only major problem was over who was to dance the next to last variation, since it was without question that La Taglioni would have the honored last position. It was settled according to age. Taglioni was 41, Cerito was 28, Grisi 26 and Grahn 24. They performed their variations in reverse order beginning with the youngest.

Their costumes were of the Romantic style made famous in "La Sylphide". They wore long billowy muslin dresses with circlets of flowers on their heads. Cerito wore her flowers beside the low bun at the back of her head and Taglioni wore her pearl jewelry.

The actual choreography has been lost to us, but through study of the writings by people who saw the performances and the lithographs of Chalon which caught the poses, costumes, style and characteristics of the dancers involved, the ballet has been reconstructed, first in 1936 by Keith Lester for the Markova-Dolin Ballet and later in 1941 by Anton Dolin for Ballet Theatre.

Divertissement. The ballet begins with the ballerinas posed around Taglioni as seen in the most famous of Chalon's lithographs of the ballet. As they move, their gestures of affection and respect for each other deny any jealousy they feel.

At the end of the opening movement, the stage is left to Lucile Grahn for the first variation which is a lively allegro. Since the Danes were, and are, known for their clean footwork, this solo is full of batterie and a long series of entrechats. After she takes her bows, Grahn graciously introduces Grisi and leaves the stage to her.

Carlotta Grisi accepts the stage and, with vibrancy and delicacy, displays the technique that made her famous. Her dainty solo moves with the controlled allegro needed for the series of slow, traveling fouettés at the end. She takes her bows and exits, leaving the stage momentarily empty.

A sweet moment now as Taglioni, the oldest, and Grahn, the youngest, enter and perform a brief pas de deux. They pose to introduce Cerito for her variation.

Fanny Cerito dances to a waltz with many balancés en tournant and posés. This solo, using the graceful, fluid style of the music, may capture Cerito's charm. Her exit is noted by a grand jeté into the wings.

Cerito bows and with gracious port de bras, introduces Taglioni onto the stage. Marie Taglioni was known for her lightness and effortless dancing. Her solo is full of sustained posés in arabesque and marked by the quality that only comes from a mature artist.

Pas De Quatre

The final movement of this little ballet is performed by all four of the ballerinas who display the virtuosity of high leaps in a brisk tempo. It is also noted for a series of échappés done in a moving circle with the ladies holding hands and facing outward. At the end of this ensemble piece, the dancers resume the opening pose.

Coppélia

Music: Léo Delibes
Choreography: Arthur Saint-Léon
Book: Charles Nuitter and Arthur Saint-Léon
after a story by E.T.A. Hoffmann, "Der Sandmann"
First presented: May 25, 1870, Paris Opéra,
with Giuseppina Bozacchi as Swanilda and Eugenie Fiocre as Franz

Ballet in three acts. Ballet considers this one of its major comedies. Some consider Delibes to be the first great ballet composer, followed by Tchaikovsky. This ballet is based on E.T.A. Hoffmann's story "Der Sandmann" which also provides the basis for the first act of the opera, "Tales of Hoffmann".

ACT I. The scene opens on the village square in a European town many years ago. Swanilda, the prettiest girl in the village, is engaged to the handsome Franz, but lately his attention has been toward the lovely girl who sits on the balcony of Dr. Coppélius' house across the way. Swanilda enters and, trying to make friends with her, waves hello. But she can't get the girl to even smile at her. She just sits there reading her book. Swanilda stamps her foot and begins to leave when she hears Franz coming and she hides. Franz has also tried to get the girl's attention and has thrown kisses up to her. But the only attention he has gotten is from Swanilda who is not happy with his attention to the girl on the balcony. Swanilda returns pretending to chase a butterfly. Franz catches it and pins it to his shirt. Swanilda cries at his thoughtless gesture and accuses him of not loving her. Franz tries to tell Swanilda that he does truly love her. Not believing him, she runs off just as a group of villagers enter. They engage Franz in a merry mazurka.

As the dancing ends, the Burgomaster enters and announces that there is to be a big festival celebrating the arrival of the new town bell and that any couple wishing to be married on that day will receive a special dowry. The Burgomaster asks Swanilda if she will be wed, but since she is unsure of Franz, she will believe what the ear of wheat tells her. Legend says that if the ear of wheat rattles, love is true, but if there is no sound, love is not. Swanilda and Franz dance and shake the ear of wheat. Swanilda hears no sound. She is heartbroken. Franz shakes the ear of wheat and says he hears the rattle, but Swanilda doesn't believe him. So the engagement is broken and Swanilda goes off in one direction and Franz in the other. The rest of the villagers stay to dance a czardas, a Hungarian folk dance.

After the townsfolk leave, Dr. Coppélius, the toymaker, leaves his house, locks the door and is on his way. Suddenly, some pranksters appear and begin to tease and jostle Dr. Coppélius. He runs them off threatening them with his cane. After they are gone, he pulls out his kerchief and wipes his brow as he totters on his way. But he has accidentally dropped his key.

Swanilda and her friends pass Dr. Coppélius' house and discover the key on the ground. Swanilda persuades her friends to follow her into Dr. Coppélius' house and confront the girl inside who ignores everyone and only reads her book. Just after they have all entered the house, Franz,

Coppélia

who has had the same idea, comes to Dr. Coppélius' house with a ladder. He intends to climb up to the balcony and get into the house from there. But Dr. Coppélius runs in, for he has now discovered that his key is missing. He chases Franz away, turns and sees his front door standing open. Dr. Coppélius rushes into his house as Franz, still determined, re-enters and starts to climb up his ladder once again as the curtain closes.

ACT II. This act takes place inside Dr. Coppélius' workroom. Swanilda and her friends have entered a very mysterious room where there are several people around, but no one moves or says hello. One of the friends stumbles over something and suddenly there is movement. The friends look closer and realize that this is a mechanical doll, a Chinese doll that dances. They soon have all the other dolls wound up and dancing around. Swanilda looks behind the curtains of an alcove. Inside is the lovely girl who only reads her book. This is Coppélia and she, too, is a doll! The friends are laughing and dancing with the dolls when suddenly Dr. Coppélius appears. He is furious and chases the girls out. But Swanilda hides inside the alcove.

As Dr. Coppélius begins to straighten the dolls up and put things back in order, he hears a noise. Franz has climbed up and is sneaking through the window. Dr. Coppélius, realizing that this may be his chance to test his magic, surprises him. Instead of chasing him off, he offers Franz some wine, to which he has added a special potion. Soon Franz falls asleep in the chair. Now Dr. Coppélius can cast his spell from his Big Book of Spells.

He goes to the alcove and rolls Coppélia out into the room. Swanilda has changed clothes with the doll and sits just like the real Coppélia does with her book. Dr. Coppélius reads from his Big Book of Spells and goes over to Franz. Believing with all his heart that he can pull life out of Franz,

he carefully carries it over to his beloved Coppélia and gently gives it to her.

Suddenly, Coppélia stands up. He rushes back over to Franz and pulls more life from him and gives it to Coppélia. Slowly she begins to come to life. Dr. Coppélius is in ecstasy. He teaches her to dance; then like a willful child, she explores the room finding the other dolls. Dr. Coppélius shows her the mantilla from the Spanish doll and she dances a bolero with it. Then, with the plaid from the Scottish doll, she dances a Highland fling. Bored with this, she goes to his Big Book of Spells and begins kicking the pages with her toes. She runs around the room and, while Dr. Coppélius is distracted, rushes over to Franz and shakes him to wake him up. Franz does awaken and Swnailda tells him what has been going on. She and Franz cause pandemonium by winding up all the dolls and turning over the furniture before they run out of the house. Poor Dr. Coppélius is left in chaos, and his heart is broken when he discovers the lifeless body of the doll, Coppélia, as the curtain closes.

ACT III. The scene is outdoors in a meadow. This is the Festival of the Bell, and Swanilda and Franz are to be married. Dr. Coppélius enters interrupting the festivities and angrily tells of the destruction and heartbreak they caused him. Swanilda, feeling very guilty and sorry for the old man, offers him her dowry to pay for the damages. But the Lord of the Manor tells Swanilda to keep her dowry and gives a bag of gold to Dr. Coppélius instead.

As the pageant begins there is a series of divertissements which may include the Dance of the Hours, Dawn, and Prayer. And Swanilda and Franz perform their pas de deux. Then the corps de ballet joins in and dances with joy and happiness to end the ballet.

La Bayadère

Music: Alois Ludwig Minkus
Choreography: Marius Petipa
Libretto: Sergei Khudekov and Marius Petipa
Sets and Costumes: I. Andreyev, M. Bocharov, P. Lambin, A. Roller, M. Shishkov, and H. Wagner
First presented: January 23, 1877, Maryinsky Theatre, St. Petersburg with Ekaterina Vazem as Nikia, Pavel Gerdt, Lev Ivanov, Maria
Gorshenkova and Maria M. Petipa

Ballet in four acts. In India a bayadère is a temple dancer. This ballet was one of Petipa's major successes at the Imperial Theatre. Today, credit for character listings differ, although they agree that Ekaterina Vazem was the first Nikia. But the practice of splitting roles during the evening has caused some conflict. Some sources state that Pavel Gerdt did the dancing part of the role of Solar, while Lev Ivanov did the acting/mime part of the role. Other sources credit Ivanov as the Rajah. Then there is the role of Gamsatti where some credit Maria Gorshenkova and others credit Maria M. Petipa. Gorshenkova has also been credited with the role of Aija (or Aya), Gamsatti's **servant. Even though it** has remained in the repertoire of the Russian ballet, Petipa's choreography has undergone many changes. In the West, only Act IV, "The Kingdom of the Shades", was known until Natalia Makarova restaged the entire ballet for American Ballet Theatre in 1980. She reduced the four acts into three by combining the original Acts I, II and III into Act I, Scenes I, II and III. Her Act II is the "Kingdom of the Shades" and her Act III is the Wedding where she restored the onstage destruction of the temple to end the ballet. Below is Petipa's four act version.

ACT I. <u>Indian Temple.</u> Solor, a young warrior returning from a hunt, has come to offer a tiger to the Rajah. Hoping to see his beloved Nikia, a bayadère, he remains near the temple to pray over the sacred fire. Before he leaves, Solor sends a fakir to tell Nikia to meet him later. Now it is time for the ritual of the sacred fire. The Brahmins, High Priest, bayadères and dervishes all assemble and dance their various ritual dances. A Brahmin priest, in love with Nikia, makes his feelings known to her. But Nikia refuses him, for she loves Solor. Later when Solor and Nikia meet, he persuades her of his love and swears his fidelity to her by the holy fire. The Brahmin has overheard all of this and swears his revenge.

ACT II. <u>Rajah's Palace.</u> Delighted by Solor's gift, the Rajah offers Solor the hand of his daughter, Gamsatti, in marriage. Solor, afraid to refuse this powerful ruler and, captivated by Gamsatti's beauty, accepts. He has forgotten his vow to Nikia. The betrothal of Solor and Gamsatti is celebrated by the Rajah's court dancers performing the Jampé dance. The Brahmin uses this opportunity to tell the Rajah of the vows between Solor and Nikia, which is overheard by Gamsatti. Nikia is summoned to Gamsatti who tells her the name of her betrothed. Refusing to believe that Solor would break his vow to her, Nikia attacks Gamsatti, but is restrained by the servant Aija. Gamsatti decides that Nikia must be killed.

ACT III. <u>Wedding.</u> Nikia must dance with the other bayadères during the wedding of Solor and Gamsatti. Ajia hands her a basket of flowers to dance with, in which is hidden a poisonous snake. Nikia is bitten. The Brahmin offers a vial with an antidote to save her if Nikia will agree to be his. She refuses him and continues to dance until she dies.

ACT IV. <u>Kingdom of the Shades.</u> Distraught over Nikia's death, Solor enters a deep sleep and finds himself among the shades (ghosts) of bayadères. This scene is one of the

La Bayadère

most famous in ballet for the work of the corps de ballet. The Shades, each dressed in a white tutu with a long scarf descending from the back of the head and attached to each arm, enter one by one, executing the famous arabesque penché combination until all (usually 36) have crisscrossed the stage in hypnotic sequence. Solor awakens from this dream and proceeds with his marriage to Gamsatti. The ceremony includes the famous dance of the Golden Idol. Just as the vows are to be taken, the gods destroy the temple, sending it crashing down on all those inside. Nikia comes for Solor and, using a long veil, guides him to Paradise.

The Sleeping Beauty

Music: Peter Ilyich Tchaikovsky
Choreography: Marius Petipa
Book: Marius Petipa and Ivan Vsevolojsky, after the fairy tale "La Belle au Bois Dormant" from "Mother Goose" by Charles Perrault
Scenery and Costumes: Ivan Vsevolojsky
First presented: January 15, 1890, Russian Imperial Ballet, Maryinsky Theatre, St. Petersburg, with Carlotta Brianza as Princess Aurora,
Paul Gerdt as Prince Florimund, Maria Petipa as the Lilac Fairy, Enrico Cecchetti as Carabosse and as the Bluebird

Ballet in prologue and three acts. This is Tchaikovsky's second ballet score. Notes from Petipa indicating he wanted so many measures of this tempo and so many of that tempo, along with exact descriptions of actions and details of emotions, guided Tchaikovsky in his composing. This close collaboration is reflected in the fact of the ballet's continued success for over one hundred years.

PROLOGUE. The curtain opens on the Great Hall of King Florestan's palace. Today his baby, Princess Aurora, is to be christened. Cattalabutte, the master of ceremonies, is rushing around making sure that everything is ready. Members of the court, dressed in their finest, enter and take their places. A fanfare announces the arrival of the King and Queen. Another fanfare announces the arrival of the fairy godmothers and their cavaliers. They are the Fairy of the Crystal Fountain, the Fairy of the Enchanted Garden, the Fairy of the Woodland Glades, the Fairy of the Songbirds, the Fairy of the Golden Vine and the most beautiful and powerful of all, the Lilac Fairy. They dance a pas de six with their partners. This is followed by each of the fairies dancing her own distinctive solo.

The fairies give their gifts to the King and Queen for the baby princess. Just as the Lilac Fairy is about to present her gift, there is a terrible noise and commotion with lightning flashes and deep rumbling sounds. An ugly rat runs into the Great Hall followed by other ugly rats pulling a coach in which the evil fairy Carabosse sits. She is furious and demands to know why she was not invited. The King grabs the guest list and discovers that Carabosse had indeed been left off. The King and Queen try to apologize for the oversight, but Carabosse's anger at being slighted is too great. She says her gift to the little princess is not a blessing but a curse, that when Aurora is sixteen she will prick her finger and die. As she steps up to the cradle, the Lilac Fairy forbids her to come any closer. Carabosse recoils and flees the Great Hall taking all the ugly rats with her. The King and Queen are horrified by this curse.

The Lilac Fairy tells them she cannot undo the curse, but she does have the power to change it. She tells them that Aurora will not die when she pricks her finger, but will sleep for one hundred years. Then a handsome prince will awaken her with a kiss of true love and they will live happily ever after. The King and Queen bow to the Lilac Fairy as the curtain closes.

ACT I. The scene opens on the celebration of Aurora's sixteenth birthday. All these years her father has ordered that sharp pointed objects are not allowed around Aurora for fear of the curse by Carabosse. But today three old hags huddle over their forbidden spindles. They are caught and brought before the King who is ready to hand out harsh punishment, but the Queen is touched by their age and asks for mercy. The King relents, for it is Aurora's birthday celebration.

The Sleeping Beauty

The festivities begin and peasant girls waltz and weave patterns with flower garlands as they dance. Aurora enters and greets her guests. The King introduces the four foreign princes who have come to seek her hand in marriage. They dance the famous "Rose Adagio", so named for the roses they present to Aurora. This is followed by other dances by Aurora and her friends.

As Aurora dances by, one of the old hags offers her a gift for her birthday. Aurora is delighted and begins playing with it. It is a spindle and as predicted, she pricks her finger on it. The old hag cackles horribly and reveals herself to be Carabosse. The Lilac Fairy appears as attendants carry Aurora to her bedchamber for the long sleep. With the wave of her magic wand, the Lilac Fairy casts the sleeping spell over the whole court. As the curtain slowly closes, the stage darkens and vines and great branches entwine to hide the palace for the duration of the sleep.

ACT II. One hundred years have passed. The curtain opens on a forest where the hunting party of Prince Florimund is nearby. Several dances and games take place to entertain the group. Later that evening as the Prince walks alone, the Lilac Fairy appears to him and tells him of the sleeping beauty. She tells him that only the kiss of a prince who will truly love her will awaken her from this curse. Intrigued, he asks the Lilac Fairy if he may see her. She shows him a vision of Princess Aurora, and Prince Florimund falls in love with her immediately. The Prince asks the Lilac Fairy to show him the way to her and they begin their journey to the palace as the curtain closes.

ACT III, SCENE I. The scene begins by showing the overgrowth of vines and cobwebs that cover the once wondrous palace. All is quiet and safe there. With the Lilac Fairy's help, Prince Florimund finds the sleeping princess. He kisses her tenderly and she awakens. The lights grow dim as the magic of theatre now restores the palace to its proper splendor.

ACT III, SCENE II. The lights come up and the Great Hall is once again busy with activity. The master of ceremonies, Catalabutte, is arranging the entertainment for the wedding festivities of Princess Aurora and Prince Florimund. The King and Queen enter with their courtiers and ladies. The other guests arrive and are presented to the court. A polonaise is danced and then the divertissements begin.

First is a pas de trois performed by Aurora's brother and their two sisters. This is followed by the humorous, mewing dance of the White Cat and Puss in Boots. Next comes the famous Bluebird Pas de Deux performed by the Enchanted Princess and the Bluebird. Little Red Riding Hood and the wolf then entertain with their dances. Now the most famous and beautiful pas de deux of the ballet is performed by Princess Aurora and Prince Florimund.

The final divertissement is the dance of the Three Ivans who perform for the bridal couple. The finale is danced by the entire company who join together for the mazurka. The curtain closes on the Prince and Princess as they are surrounded by their friends.

Swan Lake

Music: Peter Ilyich Tchaikovsky
Choreography: First incomplete staging by Julius Reisinger, March 4, 1877, Bolshoi Theatre, Moscow
Reproduced with new choreography by Lev Ivanov and Marius Petipa, February 8, 1895, Russian Imperial Ballet, Maryinsky Theatre, St. Petersburg, with Pierina Legnani as Odette-Odile.
Book: V.P. Begitchev and Vasily Geltzer
Scenery: Botcharov and Levogt

Ballet in four acts. Although this is Tchaikovsky's first ballet score, very little of it was used in the first presentation. The Moscow staging was a dismal attempt and another composer's music was used. Tchaikovsky was not happy with his score anyway, and had intended to rewrite it, but never did. Nor did he ever see the Ivanov/Petipa version, for he died in 1893. This ballet, with its challenging, dramatic dual roles of Odette-Odile, is one most female dancers wish to dance at least once. It is sometimes considered the mark by which a dancer receives the title "ballerina". Legnani, the Italian ballerina of the Russian Imperial Ballet, injected her famous thirty-two fouettés into the coda of the Black Swan Pas de Deux and they have remained in the choreography ever since.

ACT I. In the palace garden, friends have gathered to honor Prince Siegfried's twenty-first birthday. His closest friend, Benno, and his old tutor, Wolfgang, are there along with other guests from the surrounding areas. The Prince's mother enters and tells Siegfried that because he is now of age, he must choose a wife. She has arranged a formal ball for the following evening at which he must select his future wife from the eligible maidens to be presented to him. The Prince is unhappy at this news and no longer seems to enjoy the party. Benno, understanding the feelings of his friend, sees a flock of swans flying overhead and suggests that a hunt would cheer him up. The Prince agrees and orders the preparations. Crossbows in hand, the curtain closes as the hunting party goes off into the woods.

ACT II. The scene opens as the hunting party arrives near a lake where the swans were spotted to have landed. The hunters separate to seek various vantage points along the lakeside. As Prince Siegfried is about to leave, the most beautiful woman he has ever seen enters, but she also appears to be part swan. She preens like a bird, but yet looks like a woman. As he approaches her, she is terrified and trembles. He assures her he will not harm her and asks who she is. Through classic pantomime she tells him she is Odette, Queen of the Swans. The lake was made from her mother's tears because she and her maidens were put under a spell by the evil magician, Von Rothbart, and swans they must remain except between midnight and dawn. The spell can only be broken if a man loves her and remains faithful to only her. Siegfried has fallen in love with Odette and swears to her that he is that man. Suddenly Von Rothbart appears. Odette pleads with him not to harm Siegfried and begs Siegfried not to shoot Von Rothbart with his crossbow. But Von Rothbart has disappeared. Siegfried asks Odette to come to the ball the next evening so he can pick her as his bride. Odette tells him that she is restricted by the spell, but to be careful because Von Rothbart will try to make him break his vow. The lovers leave for a walk in the forest.

Benno and the other hunters return looking for Siegfried. A noise alerts them that the swans are close by. They hide in the bushes with their crossbows aimed. Beautiful white

Swan Lake

swans enter and dance as they crisscross the stage. But at the sudden approach of the hunters from their hiding places, the swans huddle together in fear. Suddenly, Prince Siegfried runs in and orders the hunters to put down their crossbows as the Swan Queen rushes in to protect her flock. Siegfried tells the huntsmen of the sad tale, and in respect they bow to the maidens. The corps de ballet dance and end poised in groupings around the stage. Siegfried and Odette perform their beautiful pas de deux aided by Benno. This is followed by the famous precision dance, the cygnets pas de quatre, or dance of the little swans. There is more dancing by the swan maidens before Odette returns for a lovely solo. But the light of dawn approaches and Von Rothbart appears and calls Odette and the swans to their flight. As the curtain closes, Prince Siegfried, Benno and the hunters watch helplessly as they pass overhead.

ACT III. In the Great Hall of the castle there has been much preparation for the formal ball tonight. The guests begin to arrive. Six girls are presented and dance for the Prince, but he is not interested in any of them. His mother reminds him that he must choose a bride tonight. The Prince, thinking only of Odette, dances obligingly with each of the maidens. An unexpected guest arrives with his daughter, Odile, who is dressed in black. The Prince is stunned by her likeness to his beloved Odette and invites her for a walk in the garden. Von Rothbart, pleased with his daughter's achievement so far, turns his charm on the prince's mother. She invites him to sit with her and watch the divertissements prepared for the court's entertainment.

They include a Spanish dance, a Hungarian czardas and a Polish mazurka.

Siegfried and Odile return and, during the celebrated Black Swan Pas de Deux, Odile bewitches him. Siegfried, unaware of the real Odette fluttering in the window trying to warn him, is so enraptured and certain she is Odette, that he asks for her hand in marriage. The evil Von Rothbart makes him swear his oath. Siegfried does, thinking it is to Odette. Von Rothbart and his daughter, Odile, reveal themselves with terrible laughter at having made Siegfried break his vow to be faithful to Odette. The Prince realizes the horrible turn of events just as he sees the helpless, fluttering Odette in the window. Siegfried is in despair as the curtain closes.

ACT IV. Again the scene is by the lake where the swan maidens comfort Odette. Siegfried seeks her out from among the swans surrounding her and vows that his love for her is eternal. Odette has forgiven Siegfried because he was tricked. But because of her betrayal, the evil magician has won and her only release from the spell now is through her death. To be free to love him forever, Odette throws herself into the lake and drowns. Siegfried, knowing he does not want to live without her, willingly follows her into death. This act of true love destroys the evil Von Rothbart and frees the swan maidens from their curse. In the final tableau the swan corps de ballet bows farewell to their queen, as the images of Odette and Siegfried pass over the lake.

The Ballet Book

Anatomy

Anatomy

There are many parts to our bodies, and each of these parts fits into its own group, forming a system. Our bodies are made up of several systems:

1   Brain - control center of the body

2   Circulatory system - carries needed fuels to all parts of the body

3   Digestive system - produces some of the body's needed fuels and carries solid waste out of the body

4   Muscular system - enables the body to move

5   Nervous system - tells the brain what's happening

6   Reproductive system - used in having babies

7   Respiratory system - produces different fuels also needed by the body

8   Skeletal system - provides the bone framework

9   Urinary system - carries liquid waste out of the body

For now we will concentrate only on the skeletal system.

Skeleton

There are over 200 bones in the human frame and this skeleton supports the entire weight of the body. Some places of the body are serviced by just one bone as in the upper-arm bone, called the humerus. But in other places there are many more; for instance, 26 bones in each foot, 27 bones in each hand, 24 ribs, and 33 vertebrae.

The Skull

The skull, or head, is above the very top vertebra, called the atlas. It provides a thick, protective layer over the soft brain tissues that control the eyes, ears, nose and mouth and the delicate functions of thinking, learning, speaking and so on.

The Spine

The largest set of bones that are fitted together forms the main support of the skeleton, called the backbone or spinal column. This column also houses and protects the main nerve, or spinal cord, which starts from the brain and runs down through this canal.

An individual bone of the backbone is called a vertebra. As a group they are called vertebrae. A spongy cartilage pad cushions each vertebra as it does many other bones. This prevents one bone rubbing against another during movement. Of the 33 vertebrae, the lowest 4 are fused together to form the coccyx, or tailbone. Attached above the coccyx is another set of 5 fused vertebrae called the sacrum.

The spine has 4 curves which act as additional shock absorbers:

Cervical - The small inward curve at the back of the neck is made up of 7 vertebrae

Thoracic - Curving outward, these 12 vertebrae are where the ribs are attached

Lumbar - Reversing the curve inward again, these 5 are the largest vertebrae and form the "hollow" of the back

Sacrum - Curving outward and slightly under, these are the 9 fused vertebrae of the sacrum and coccyx

The Ribs

A barrel shaped chest cavity (thoracic cavity) protects vital organs like the heart, lungs and others. This is made up of 12 pairs of curved ribs. The top 7 pairs are attached to the breastbone, or sternum, in front. The next 3 pairs are attached by cartilage to the rib immediately above and the remaining 2 pairs are unattached, sometimes called floating ribs.

The Arms and Legs

The skeleton has two wide parts known as girdles. These are the shoulder girdle and the hip girdle. The shoulder girdle is attached to the sternum, and the hip girdle is attached to the backbone.

The shoulder girdle has on each side a collarbone (clavicle) and a shoulder blade (scapu-

la). Attached to it is the upper-arm bone (humerus) followed by the lower-arm bones (radius and ulna) to which is then attached the hand with its 27 bones. The hand's numerous bones are divided into the following: 8 carpals (wrist), 5 metacarpals (palm) and 14 phalanges (fingers).

The hip or pelvic girdle, shaped like a bowl, is formed by the hipbone. Each side has a socket into which fits the thighbone, or femur, the largest bone in the body. Below the femur is the knee cap (patella), where the knee joint is formed by the thighbone (femur) and the leg bone (tibia). Attached at the end of the lower leg bones (tibia and fibula) is the area called the ankle where then extends the 26 bones of the foot. These are the 7 tarsals (ankle), 5 metatarsals (arch) and 14 phalangs (toes).

Ligaments and Tendons

Ligament, from the Latin word "ligare," means to bind or tie. The function of ligaments is to hold the bones together, maintaining the stability of the skeletal structure. Although they are somewhat pliable, they are not considered elastic nor easily stretched. Once they are stretched, which takes a long period of time, they cannot return to their original length. Ligaments join bone to bone.

A tendon, or sinew, is made of inelastic fibrous tissues forming a tough cord or band. The most familiar tendon to a dancer is the Achilles, which is the common tendon of the calf muscles in the back of the ankle. Tendons join muscle to bone.

Skeleton (Front)

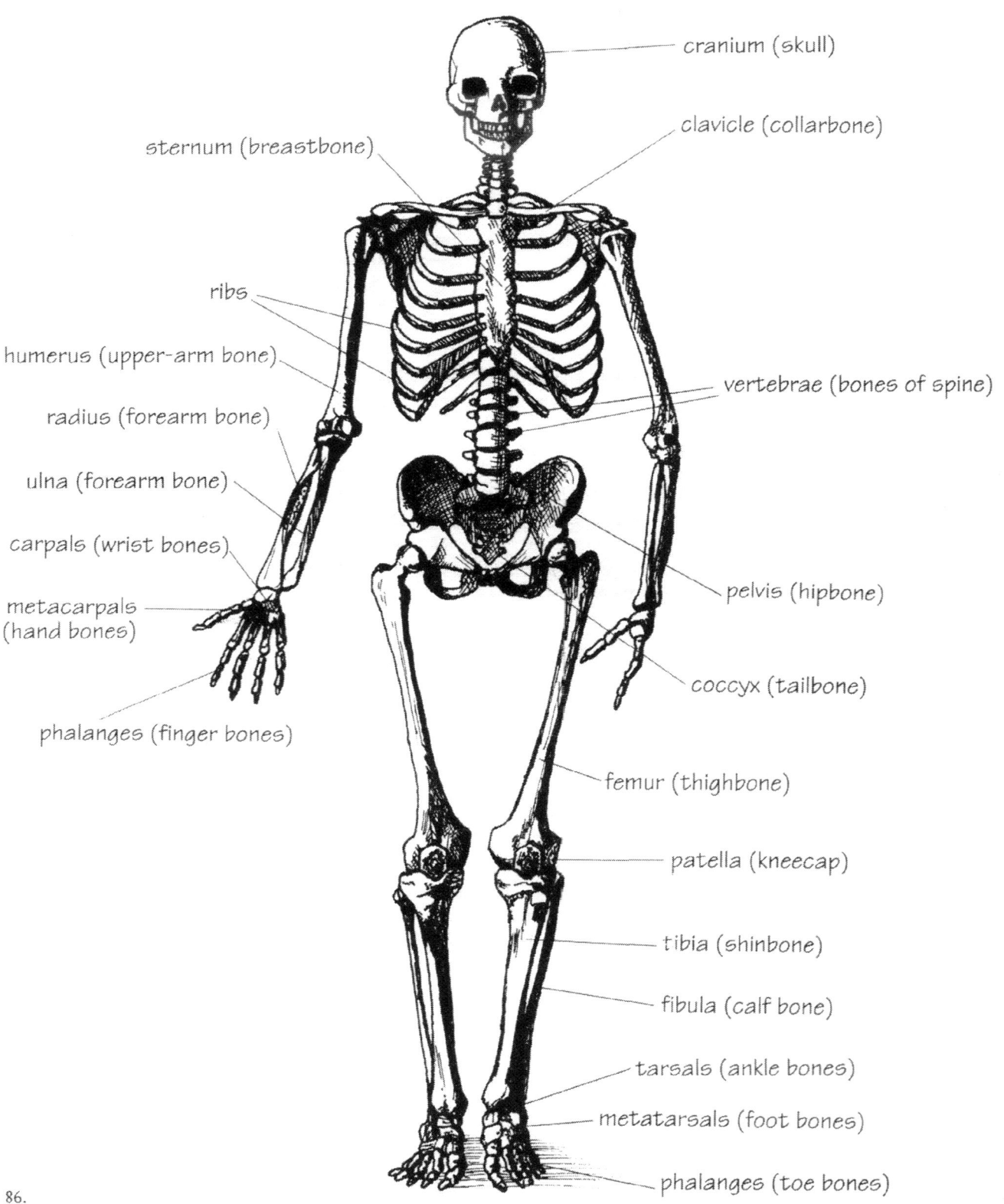

cranium (skull)

clavicle (collarbone)

sternum (breastbone)

ribs

humerus (upper-arm bone)

radius (forearm bone)

ulna (forearm bone)

carpals (wrist bones)

metacarpals
(hand bones)

phalanges (finger bones)

vertebrae (bones of spine)

pelvis (hipbone)

coccyx (tailbone)

femur (thighbone)

patella (kneecap)

tibia (shinbone)

fibula (calf bone)

tarsals (ankle bones)

metatarsals (foot bones)

phalanges (toe bones)

Skeleton (Back)

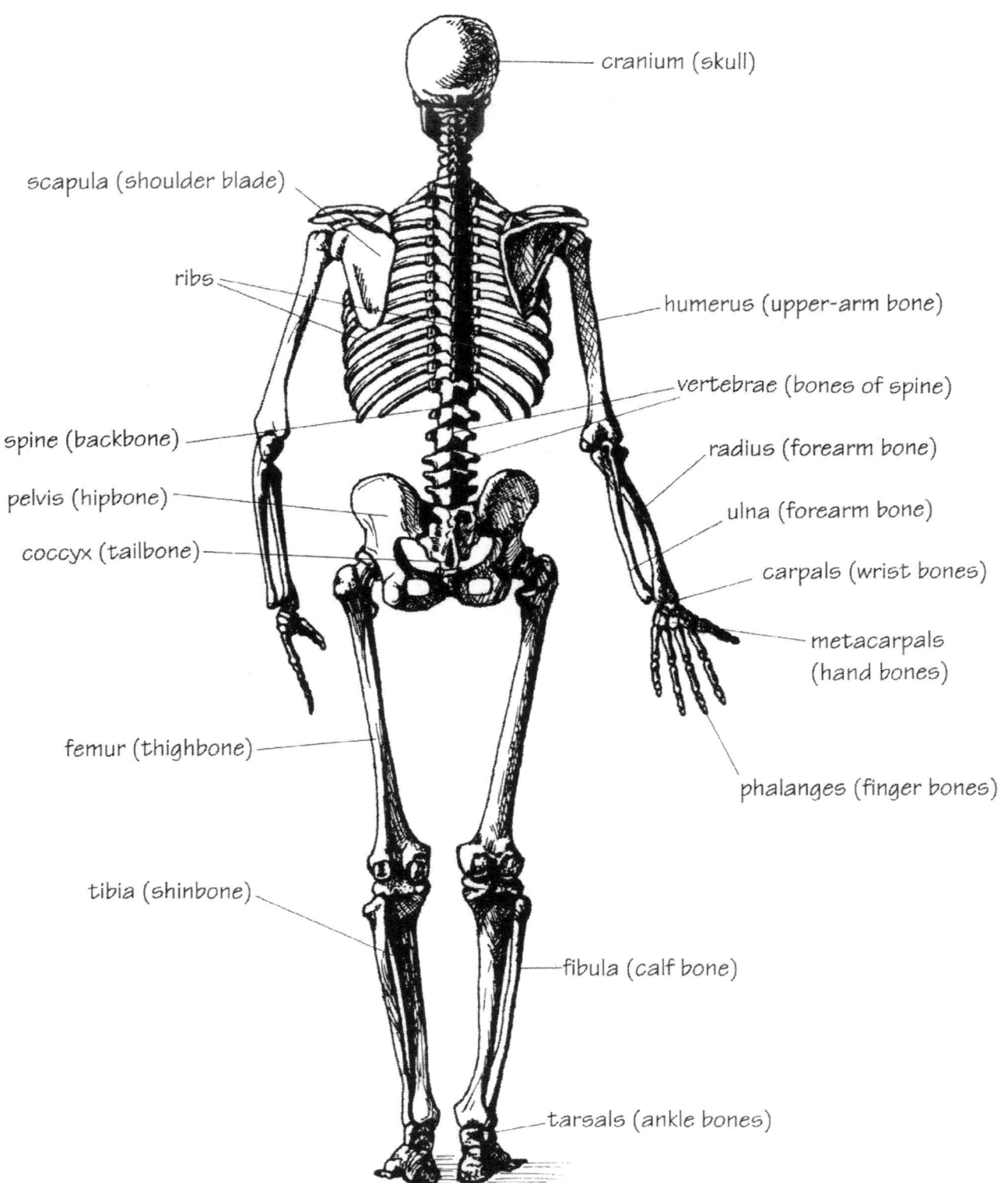

cranium (skull)

scapula (shoulder blade)

ribs

humerus (upper-arm bone)

vertebrae (bones of spine)

spine (backbone)

radius (forearm bone)

pelvis (hipbone)

ulna (forearm bone)

coccyx (tailbone)

carpals (wrist bones)

metacarpals
(hand bones)

femur (thighbone)

phalanges (finger bones)

tibia (shinbone)

fibula (calf bone)

tarsals (ankle bones)

The Ballet Book

Vocabulary

Vocabulary

à la seconde (ah la seh-GAWND)
to the second

à terre (ah TERE)
on the ground

adage (ah DAHZH)
at ease, leisure

allégro (ah-LAY-grow)
lively, brisk

arabesque (air-ra-BESK)
name of a Moorish ornament, longest line the
body can make from fingertips to toes

assemblé (ah-som-BLAY)
assembled, joined together

attitude (at-te-TUDE)
a position standing on one leg with the other
leg lifted, bent at the knee

au milieu (oh mel-YOU)
in the middle or center

balancé (ba-lan-SAY)
rocking

ballerina (bal-ah-REE-nah)
female dancer

ballet (bal-LAY)
an artistic dance in which music, movement
and mime are used as part of a theatrical
performance often suggesting a story, idea
or mood

ballon (ba-LAWN)
balloon, light, ball-like bounce

barre (bahr)
bar

battement (bat-MAW)
beating

battement frappé (bat-MAW fra-PAY)
struck beating

bourrée (boo-RAY)
series of quick little steps in fifth position
relevé, changing weight from one foot to the
other, traveling in any direction

bras (bra)
arms

bras bas (bra BAH)
arms low

chaînés (sha-NAY)
chains, links

changement (shahnzh-MAW)
change

chassé (sha-SAY)
chase

choreography (co-ree-OG-ra-fee)
steps, patterns, designs of movement for a
ballet or dance composition

corps de ballet (core duh bal-LAY)
a body of dancers who dance in groups
forming the "chorus" of a ballet

cou-de-pied (coo-duh-PYAY)
neck of the foot (ankle)

coupé (coo-PAY)
 cut, cutting

couru (coo-REW)
 running

croisé (krwah-ZAY)
 crossed

de face (duh FAHSS)
 full face front

dégagé (day-ga-ZHAY)
 disengaged

demi (de-MEE)
 half

demi-contretemps (de-MEE-con-tra-TAHN)
 half against time

derrière (deh-ree-YAIR)
 behind

devant (duh-VAHN)
 front

développé (dev-la-PAY)
 to unfold

écarté (ay-car-TAY)
 wide apart

échappé (ay-sha-PAY)
 escaping

effacé (ef-fa-SAY)
 shaded

élancé (ay-lahn-SAY)
 darting

élévation (el-la-vay-SHAWN)
 raising, lifting, loftiness - the ability of a
 dancer to attain height in dancing

en (ahn)
 in

en arrière (ahn a-ree-YAIR)
 backward

en avant (ahn a-VAHN)
 forward

en bas (ahn BAH)
 in low

en croix (ahn KRWAH)
 in the shape of a cross

en dedans (ahn duh-DAHN)
 inward

en dehors (ahn duh-OAR)
 outward

en diagonale (ahn dy-yag-ga-NAL)
 in the diagonal

en haut (ahn OH)
 on high

en l'air (ahn LAIR)
 in the air

en promenade (ahn prom-NOD)
 in a walk, walking

enchaînement (ahn-shay-MAW)
 linking, chaining

épaulé (ay-poh-LAY)
 shouldered

étendre (ay-TEHN-dra)
  to stretch

extension (ex-ten-SHAWN)
  the ability of a dancer to raise and hold an
  extended leg en l'air

fermé (fehr-MAY)
  close

fondu (fawn-DEW)
  melting

fouetté (fweh-TAY)
  whipped

frappé (frah-PAY)
  struck

glissade (glee-SAHD)
  glide

grand (grahn)
  big, large

grand battement (grahn bat-MAW)
  big beating

grand jeté (grahn zheh-TAY)
  big throw

jeté (zheh-TAY)
  thrown

pas (pah)
  step

pas de basque (pah duh BASK)
  Basque step, from folk dances of the Basque
  region between France and Spain

pas de bourrée (pah duh boo-RAY)
  series of three steps done in any direction
  and/or turning. The most common is step
  behind on left, step side on right, close left
  in front of right foot in fifth position

pas de chat (pah duh SHA)
  step of the cat

pas de deux (pah duh DUH)
  step of two, dance for two

passé (pa-SAY)
  pass

petit (peh-TEE)
  little, small

piqué (pee-KAY)
  pricked

pirouette (pier-WET)
  whirl or spin

plié (plee-ay)
  bent, bending

pointe tendue (pwent tahn-DEW)
  point stretched

port de bras (pour duh BRA)
  carriage of the arms

posé (poh-ZAY)
  poised

premier danseur (pre-MEER dan-SUR)
  first dancer, male

préparation (prey-pa-ray-SHAWN)
  preparation

quatrième (ca-tree-EM)
  fourth

relevé (rel-a-VAY)
  raised

retiré (reh-tee-RAY)
  retired, withdrawn

révérence (rev-ah-RAHNS)
  curtsy, bow

rond (ron)
  round

rond de jambe (ron duh zham)
  round of the leg

sans changer (sahn shahn-ZHAY)
  without change

sauté (so-TAY)
  jumped, jumping

soubresaut (soo-bra-SEW)
  spring, bound

sous-sus (soo-SEW)
  under-over

soutenu (soot-NEW)
  sustained

sur (sir)
  on, upon

temps (tahn)
  time

temps levé (tahn luh-VAY)
  time raised

temps lié (tahn lee-ay)
  connected movement

tendu (tahn-DEW)
  stretched

Terpsichore (Turp-SICK-o-ree)
  the Greek muse of dance

tour (toor)
  turn

turn-out (tern-out)
  the 90-degree position of the feet and legs
  obtained by rotating the leg from inside the
  hip joint

tutu (too-too)
  the classical skirt worn by female dancers
  made of many layers of net, a short skirt
  or calf-length romantic skirt

variation (var-yay-SHAWN)
  referring to a solo dance

The Ballet Book

Answers

Answers

Lesson One
1. See drawing at right.
2. See drawing at right.
   Explanation: To get a classical, clean line of the body.
3. French, Italian, Russian
4. (a) earthy, sensual (b) Marie Taglioni, Dr. Véron
5. The Italian "ballare"
6. the first ballet
7. (a) 1786, Bordeaux, France (b) Lisette, Colin (c) mother
8. (a) True (b) metatarsals, hand bones
9. From top to bottom - 3, 1, 4, 2
10. See the Vocabulary Directory

1.

2.

Audience		
8	1	2
7	Dancer	3
6	5	4

RUSSIAN VAGANOVA METHOD

Audience		
	5	
6	Dancer	8
	7	

ITALIAN CECCHETTI METHOD

Lesson Two
1. See Theory section for what your school uses.
2. (a) "La Sylphide", La Taglioni (b) ethereal
3. Thoinot Arbeau, 1588
4. "Sun King", 1669, Paris Opéra Ballet
5. (a) 1832, Marie Taglioni (b) Philippe
6. James, Effie, Gurn, Madge
7. Scarf
8. (a) finger, toe (b) ankle
9. From top to bottom - 2, 4, 3, 1
10. See the Vocabulary Directory

Lesson Three
1. See drawing at right.
2. (a) Jules Perrot, "Giselle" (b) "Pas de Quatre"
3. Gaetan Vestris - father, Auguste Vestris - son
4. Marie Camargo
5. Marie Sallé
6. (a) June 28, 1841, Paris Opéra (b) Carlotta Grisi (Giselle), Lucien Petipa (Albrecht), Adèle Dumilâtre (Myrtha) (c) True
7. Skeleton
8. Head - skull
9. From top to bottom - 3, 1, 4, 2
10. See the Vocabulary Directory

Center Line

1.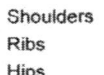

Shoulders
Ribs
Hips

Lesson Four
1. Inside the hips
2. Pull-up
3. (a) 1870 (b) "The Sleeping Beauty", "The Nutcracker", "Swan Lake" (c) Lev Ivanov, "The Nutcracker", "Swan Lake"
4. Jean Georges Noverre
5. Dancing on pointe - "La Sylphide"
6. 1892, E.T.A. Hoffmann
7. Snow Scene: Act I, Scene II \ Kingdom of Sweets: Act II \ Christmas Party: Act I, Scene I
8. Femur, coccyx
9. From top to bottom - 2, 1, 4, 3
10. See the Vocabulary Directory

Lesson Five

1. A
2. (a) Carlotta Grisi (b) "Pas de Quatre"
3. The long white tutu.
4. Augusta Maywood
5. (a) Taglioni, Grisi, Cerito, Grahn (b) age
6. 2
7. 2
8. 24
9. From top to bottom - 4, 3, 1, 2
10. See the Vocabulary Directory

Lesson Six

1. See Theory Section for what your school uses
2. (a) "Coppélia" (b) colorful, local realism highlighted by lively folk dances.
3. Code of Terpsichore, 1830, Carlo Blasis
4. 1735
5. (a) E.T.A. Hoffmann (b-1) True (b-2) False (b-3) True (b-4) True
6. Léo Delibes
7. Carpals
8. Pelvis, femur
9. From top to bottom - 4, 1, 2, 3
10. See the Vocabulary Directory

Lesson Seven

1. See Theory Section
2. (a) Arthur Saint-Léon (b) "Pas de Quatre", 1845
3. "The Sleeping Beauty" or "The Nutcracker" or "Swan Lake"
4. Charles-Louis Didelot, father
5. (a) 1877 (b) Solor, Nikia, Gamsatti
6. Ghosts
7. Vertebrae, 4
8. Knee cap
9. From top to bottom - 1, 2, 3, 4
10. See the Vocabulary Directory

Lesson Eight

1. See drawing at right.
2. (a) Copenhagen, Denmark, Danish
   (b) "Pas de Quatre" (c) Richard Wagner's
3. Mathilde Kschessinska
4. (a) January 15, 1890 (b) Charles Perrault (c) second
5. Aurora
6. Carabosse, Blue Bird
7. Upper-arm
8. Spinal cord
9. From top to bottom - 3, 1, 4, 2
10. See the Vocabulary Directory

1.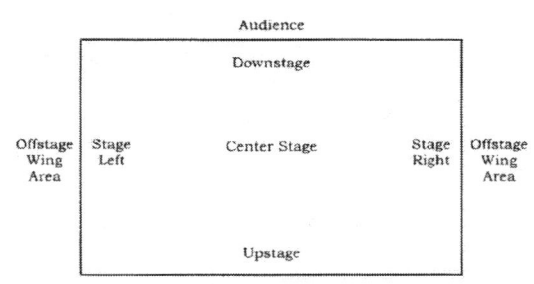

Lesson Nine

1. Turn-out, Pull-up, Placement
2. (a) Grand battement (b) 2nd position demi plié
3. (a) 1880, 1890 (b) prima ballerina assoluta
4. 1848-1858 Jules Perrot \ 1859-1870 Arthur Saint-Léon \ 1870-1903 Marius Petipa
5. (a) Odette, Odile (b) tears
6. February 8, 1895
7. Sternum, breastbone
8. Clavicle, scapula
9. From top to bottom - 2, 3, 4, 1
10. See the Vocabulary Directory

Bibliography

Balanchine, George. *Balanchine's Complete Stories Of The Great Ballets*. New York, 1954.

Balanchine, George and Mason, Francis. *101 Stories Of The Great Ballets*. New York, 1989.

Barnes, Clive. *Inside American Ballet Theatre*. New York, 1977.

Beaumont, Cyril. *Enrico Cecchetti, His Legacy To The Dance, A Brief Guide To The Origin, Amis And Objects Of The Cecchetti Method Of Training In Classical Ballet*. London, (no date).

Beaumont, Cyril W. *A Primer Of Classical Ballet (Cecchetti Method) For Children*. London, 1971.

Beaumont, Cyril W. *A Second Primer Of Classical Ballet (Cecchetti Method) For Children*. London, 1970.

Beaumont, Cyril W. *A Third Primer Of Classical Ballet (Cecchetti Method) For Children*. London, 1971.

Beaumont, Cyril W. *Complete Book Of Ballets*. New York, 1941.

Bellew, Hélène. *Ballet In Moscow Today*. Greenwich, CT/London, (no date).

Boucher, François. *20,000 Years Of Fashion*. New York, (no date).

Brockett, Oscar G. *The Theatre, An Introduction*. New York, 1964.

Bullard, Brian and Charlsen, David. *I Can Dance*. New York, 1979.

Compton's Interactive (CD-ROM) Encyclopedia. Version 1.01. 1992.

Crisp, Clement and Thorpe, Edward. *The Colorful World Of Ballet*. London, 1978.

Demidov, Alexander. *The Russian Ballet Past & Present*. New York, 1977.

Doeser, Linda. *Ballet And Dance*. New York, 1977.

Dubois, Marguerite-Marie. *Larousse's French-English English-French Dictionary*. New York, 1971.

Ettinger, Tom and Jaspersohn, Bill. *My Ballet Book*. New York, 1993.

Fonteyn, Margot. *The Magic Of Dance*. New York, 1979.

Fraser, John. *Private View, Inside Baryshnikov's American Ballet Theatre*. New York, 1988.

French, Charles Engell. *Baryshnikov At Work*. New York, 1976.

Garfunkel, Trudy. *On Wings Of Joy*. New York, 1994.

Gelabert, Raoul. *Raoul Gelabert's Anatomy For The Dancer*. New York, 1964.

Gelabert, Raoul. *Raoul Gelabert's Anatomy For The Dancer, Volume 2*. New York, 1966.

Golovkina, Sophia N. *The Bolshoi Ballet School*. U.S.A., 1987.

Grant, Gail. *Technical Manual And Dictionary Of Classical Ballet*. New York, 1967, 1982.

Grieg, Valerie. *Inside Ballet Technique*. Princeton, 1994.

Gruen, John. *The Private World Of Ballet*. New York, 1975.

Haskell, Arnold. *Ballet In Color*. New York, 1959.

Haskell, Arnold. *The Wonderful World Of Dance*. New York, 1960.

Isadora, Rachel. *My Ballet Class*. New York, 1980.

Jessel, Camilla. *Life At The Royal Ballet School*. New York, 1979.

Kent, Allegra with Camner, James and Constance. *The Dancers' Body Book*. New York, 1984.

Kirstein, Lincoln/Stuart, Muriel/Dyer, Carlus. *The Classic Ballet*. New York, 1951.

Krokover, Rosalyn. *The New Borzoi Book Of Ballets*. New York, 1956.

Lawson, Joan. *Beginning Ballet*. London, 1994.

Lawson, Joan. *The Story Of Ballet*. New York, 1976.

Loren, Teri. *The Dancer's Companion*. New York, 1978.

Mackie, Joyce. *Basic Ballet, The Steps Defined*. New York, 1980.

Mara, Thalia with Wyndham, Lee. *First Steps In Ballet*. New York, 1955.

Mara, Thalia. *Fourth Steps In Ballet: On Your Toes!* New York, 1959.

Bibliography

Massie, Suzanne. *Land Of The Firebird*. New York, 1980.

Maynard, Olga. *The American Ballet*. Philadelphia, 1959.

Messerer, Asaf. *Classes In Classical Ballet*. New York, 1972.

Money, Keith. *Fonteyn, The Making Of A Legend*. New York, 1974.

Money, Keith. *Fonteyn & Nureyev, The Great Years*. London, 1994.

The New Lexicon Webster's Encyclopedic Dictionary Of The English Language. 1990.

Nureyev, Rudolph. *Nureyev, An Autobiography*. New York, 1963.

Prince Michael of Greece. *Crown Jewels*. New York, 1986.

Reyna, Ferdinand. *Concise Encyclopedia Of Ballet*. Chicago, 1974.

Reynolds, Nancy. *Repertory In Review*. New York, 1977.

Reynolds, Nancy and Reimer-Torn, Susan. *Dance Classics*. Chicago, 1988, 1991.

Robert, Grace. *The Borzoi Book Of Ballets*. New York, 1946.

Rosenberg, Jane. *Dance Me A Story*. New York, 1985.

Tarasov, Nikolai I. *Ballet Technique For The Male Dancer*. New York, 1985.

Terry, Walter. *Ballet, A New Guide To The Liveliest Art*. New York, 1959.

Vaganova, Agrippina. *Basic Principles Of Classical Ballet, Russian Ballet Technique*. New York, 1969.

Various Contributions. *Ballet & Modern Dance*. London, 1974.

Various Contributions. *Ballet News*. New York, 1979-1982.

Various Contributions. *Dance Magazine*. New York, 1957-1995.

Various Contributions. *Dance News*. New York, 1978-1980.

Various Contributions. *The Simon And Schuster Book Of The Ballet*. New York, 1980.

Verdy, Violette. *Of Swans, Sugarplums, And Satin Slippers*. New York, 1991.

Villella, Edward with Kaplan, Larry. *Prodigal Son*. New York, 1992.

Vincent, M.D., L. M. *The Dancer's Book Of Health*. Kansas City, 1978.

Wentink, Andrew Mark. *Balletomania, A Quizzical Potpourri Of Ballet Facts, Stars, Trivia And Lore*. New York, 1980.

Western, Joan and Wilson, Ronald. *The Human Body*. New York, 1991.

Yarwood, Doreen. *European Costume, 4000 Years Of Fashion*. New York, 1982.

Index

24235179R00055

Made in the USA
Lexington, KY
10 July 2013